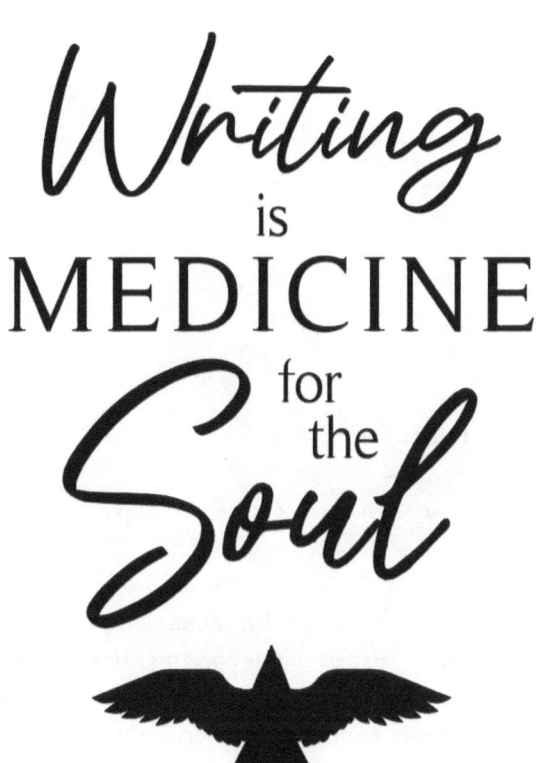

Writing is MEDICINE for the Soul

JOANNE FEDLER

Copyright © 2022 Joanne Fedler.

First produced as a course on the Insight Timer app as *Writing as Medicine for the Soul*.

All rights reserved. The author asserts her moral rights in this work through the world without waiver. No part of this book may be reproduced, or stored in a retrieval system, or transmitted in any form or by any means, electronic, mechanical, photocopying, recording or otherwise without express written permission of the publisher. For information about permission to reproduce selections from this book, write to joanne@joannefedler.com.

ISBN: 978-1-925842-41-8 (Paperback)

Joanne Fedler Media
Dolphin Street, Coogee,
2034, Australia

www.joannefedler.com

Joanne Fedler Media acknowledges the Traditional Owners and First Nations people of the land of Australia on which this book was conceived, written and published, and pays respects to Elders past, present and emerging.

For all of you

quiet writers

who long to

sing your secrets

into the bright light of

life

CONTENTS

Introduction   7

CHAPTER 1: Open a door   11

CHAPTER 2: Close the door   16

CHAPTER 3: Just believe   24

CHAPTER 4: Nurture what's here now   31

CHAPTER 5: Breathe, bathe, bake bread   38

CHAPTER 6: Give it a name   45

CHAPTER 7: Save time   53

CHAPTER 8: Release   60

CHAPTER 9: Be a lover   68

CHAPTER 10: Ask questions   75

CHAPTER 11: Catch a dream   82

CHAPTER 12: Steer   90

CHAPTER 13: Kiss the ground   97

CHAPTER 14: Trust the unknown   104

CHAPTER 15: Take a stand   112

CHAPTER 16: Let it be light   119

CHAPTER 17: Go wild	127
CHAPTER 18: Confess	134
CHAPTER 19: Play with fire	142
CHAPTER 20: Go back for the orphans	148
CHAPTER 21: Ask for help	156
CHAPTER 22: Shake the silence	163
CHAPTER 23: Remake yourself	170
CHAPTER 24: Connect the dots	178
CHAPTER 25: Switch	185
CHAPTER 26: Seek the story	193
CHAPTER 27: Make peace	200
CHAPTER 28: Offer thanks	207
CHAPTER 29: Tell the whole holy truth	215
CHAPTER 30: Make hope a habit	223
Acknowledgements	229

INTRODUCTION

As you arrive at my front door from the stairwell in our apartment building in the beachy suburb of Coogee in Sydney, you'll be greeted by a sign that reads, 'Bless this home and all who enter.'

Sometimes all we need to know is that we are welcome to enter a place, and everything changes.

Whatever constellation of circumstances have conspired to bring you here, bless you.

This book is an antidote to the pace, noise and busyness of our modern lives, and the illnesses of the spirit we all suffer from as a result.

I've been writing for many years as a professional author.

But I've also had a secret writing life that began when I was six years old and I wrote my first story, *Goodbye Kitchen*.

Writing has always been my most loyal companion.

It has helped me feel, to be raw and vulnerable, to stay connected to my heart.

It has made me painstakingly attentive and appreciative for both the ordinary and extraordinary moments that abound in any life.

It has been nourishing and therapeutic through times of loneliness, isolation and emptiness.

It keeps nudging me to ask important and difficult questions of myself and the world, and it has held my feet to the fire of my passions.

Honestly, I don't know who or where I would be without the writing I do privately in my journals, away from editors, publishers and readers.

I've also been mentoring writers for more than a decade. And I've witnessed the joy and healing that writing brings when people discover it.

The pace of our modern existence expects too much of the human heart. It exceeds our ability to process what is happening to us at an emotional, psychic and energetic level.

Writing creates the space for our souls to catch their breath. For us to spiritually digest our experiences and integrate them into the fabric of our beings.

So it is a great privilege for me to be able to share with you all the ways in which writing has kept me embodied, open and deeply grateful for every aspect of my life, including the difficult and traumatic experiences.

Writing helps us to stay connected to a greater story – one that exceeds our own small lives.

And friends, this is what all our souls cry out for. To know that we are part of something bigger than ourselves.

Writing brings us back to alignment, compassion and tenderness which serves both our individual spirits and the larger mission of caring for the entire planet on which we get to play and pray and stay as mortal beings.

We may not realize how much anguish we are holding on behalf of humanity, species and ecosystems that are imperilled.

Writing allows us to express and feel this grief.

The intimacy that grows as we put words on the page allows us to wake up to our role as guardians and caretakers of the earth.

So – no, it's not narcissistic to spend time writing, deepening, softening into your heart.

It is an act of love you bestow on everyone and everything around you.

I've designed every chapter in this book to work like a dial, a compass, a star, a lighthouse, gently nudging you back into your body and your heart.

Please have a journal, some paper, a pen with you so you're ready to flow into the writing exercise at the end of each chapter.

Most of us write on computers or devices these days, but I'm going to encourage you to consider writing by hand for the exercise in this book. Just give it a try and see how you feel. Maybe you'll rediscover the visceral sensuality of a pen in your hand and how it feels to make marks on a page through one of your unique signatures – that of your handwriting.

Maybe you'll choose a journal, a little thing of beauty with pages that feel inviting to the touch and a pen that sits with deep friendship in your hand – they are loyal collaborators and companions on a writing journey.

If this feels out of your comfort zone because you haven't picked up a pen in a long time, don't let that become an obstacle. Writing by hand is just a suggestion. Use whatever instruments or devices you're comfortable with.

This is how I've structured each chapter:
- I describe how writing can be the antidote to a particular ailment of the soul;
- I offer an affirmation or power phrase for the chapter;
- I share a practical writing skill – an element of the craft of writing – so that you leave with some practical tools;
- I give you a writing practice or prompt. Start writing for three minutes, but please feel free to continue to write for longer especially if your writing is rolling out of you.

By the end of these thirty chapters (especially if you commit to a daily practice), you'll be well on your way to making writing a habit.

I hope you will find parts of yourself that are parched and lost, so you can feed their thirst and bring them back into your loving embrace.

Come, friends.

Are you ready? Let us begin.

Chapter 1
OPEN A DOOR

The beginning is always today.
MARY SHELLEY

Imagine a door in front of you.

It's beckoning you to open it.

All you have to do is step forward, turn the handle and enter.

A doorway is a welcome, an invitation, a liminal space inviting you to move across its threshold. And your act of stepping through it marks a new beginning.

Come with me as we enter.

Now, I invite you to say, 'Here I am,' or in the words of Moses and Abraham when they were summoned by the divine, '*Hineni*.'

Hineni is Hebrew for '*Here I Am*' and it doesn't only refer to our physical 'hereness,' as in 'I'm in the room.' It has this resonance of deep spiritual readiness, the willingness to show up for whatever is being asked of us.

It's a declaration that we've put away our distractions, multi-tasking, the million options that are squealing for our attention, our dabbling here, there and everywhere; and we are fully accounted for. It's a rollcall of our entire being – body, mind, soul.

WRITING IS MEDICINE FOR THE SOUL

AFFIRMATION
'Hineni' – here I am.

Call yourself in. Beckon in your straying eye, your twitching heart, your restless soul.

See them walking through the door. Account for them.

Tick them off on the register.

Take a moment to allow yourself to arrive.

I want to welcome you here.

It's no accident that you have found yourself opening this door.

It's not a mistake. You are here to write, because some part of you knows writing is a doorway for you to connect with a part of yourself you have lost, or maybe you haven't even met yet, like Rumi's lovers, who 'don't finally meet somewhere, but have been inside each other all along.'

We write to feed a very particular kind of hunger – it's the hunger to make meaning from our lives, and to connect with our deepest selves.

It's the expression of the longing to belong somewhere and to something.

So we don't need to overanalyze it or question it too much.

What do you want? What are your intentions? Where is this relationship going? Are you really committed? Are you going to write a book?

When something arrives as a longing in our lives, let's just welcome it with curiosity.

What is this longing here to say?

Why has it shown up now?

What part of you is it awakening?

Now let's just get this out of the way: as you work your way through these chapters, please remember, there is no such thing as 'bad writing.'

What we are doing is developing a relationship of intimacy between ourselves and the page.

We're not going to worry about writing for an audience, or whether this is the start of a memoir or a novel. This is your writing journey – it is for no-one but you.

I'm not saying that it won't lead to something else – but this book is not outcome-driven or goal-oriented. I have books where I teach people to write like that and I mentor writers through the writing of books all the way to publication. But this book is not about that kind of writing.

What we write is a reflection of our consciousness at any given time.

And so the quality of our thoughts, the subtlety of our emotions and our willingness to feel them, the fine-tuning of our thinking and feeling and attention to the world – all of these precede our ability to find the exact, precise and perfect language to fix onto experiences. We have to attend to ourselves before we can think about writing for a reader.

And so this book is about this internal work that is part of any writing process.

It's sometimes called pre-writing, where we're working out deeply what we have to say before we share it with an audience.

I want to grant you the freedom to arrive at the page in all your beautiful, messy glory, without qualification or commendation. And to allow yourself to write. To write nonsense, rubbish, junk, badly, poorly, incoherently, messily. To dump whatever is in your head and set it free on the page.

If you feel as if you need permission – I'm giving it to you right here and right now.

Write yourself a permission slip if you need one.

I want you to feel uncensored, without having read any books on writing, without having passed English at school, no matter whether English is your first language or not, without any qualifications, or requirements, except the desire to write.

That's it. That's all that you need right now.

Today's chapter is about beginning. How do we begin new experiences?

Is writing a new experience for you? If so, how does that make you feel? Anxious? Nervous? Excited? A bit of both?

No matter where you are on this spectrum, this book is a new beginning – or the chance to have a new beginning.

Stop, just breathe for a moment.

You are here.

Welcome.

WRITING SKILL

One of the biggest stumbling blocks for writers is this question of 'where to begin.' This is where we can get super stuck – trying to figure out the perfect place to start.

All you need to begin is a writing prompt which I will give you at the end of each chapter.

You write it out, and you keep writing.

A writing prompt is a little nudge, a tickle in the writing ribs.

And if nothing comes to you, all you do is you rewrite the writing prompt, over and over again, until something comes to you.

Don't overthink. Just keep writing.

Use the prompt as a laxative, an invitation, a beckoning.

WRITING PROMPT
'I am here because…'

REFLECTION QUESTION

New beginnings evoke in me:
- *fear and uncertainty*
- *excitement for what may lie ahead*
- *curiosity and questions*
- *the need for closure on unfinished business before I can begin.*

NOTES

Chapter 2
CLOSE THE DOOR

Most people are other people. Their thoughts are someone else's opinions, their lives a mimicry, their passions a quotation.
OSCAR WILDE

We have become expert followers, indoctrinated into the belief that others are the measure of our success. So we also want followers and fans. We want what they're having, what's trending, fashionable, popular.

Soundbites have replaced insights.

Slogans have replaced mantras. We publicly over-share, posting our every passing thought, breakfast meal or encounter on social media, making constant announcements to the world about our lives and sometimes, our inner lives, often before we've even processed them.

As a result, we all have shorter attention spans – and so we 'live in the litter,' rather than in the 'layers,' to quote the poet Stanley Kunitz.

We fall in with the pack because – don't we all just want to be liked? To be popular? It sucks to miss out on the fun that everyone else seems to be having. FOMO (fear of missing out) is real, people.

But every now and then we might stop and ask ourselves: do I really want what I say I want?

Do I really love what I proclaim to love?

Do I really hate what I say I hate?

Don't you sometimes overhear a conversation and think to yourself, 'Seriously? How on earth can you believe that?'

Even more startling, have you ever heard yourself utter a statement and another part of you turns and whispers, 'Are you hearing yourself? Is that really true?'

In lives bombarded by media and op-ed and news we have no part in creating, we flail about in roles, social constructs, ideologies, privileges and philosophies that are so invisible and infectious, we can't tell whether we believe them or want them as part of our story.

We've become fragmented by the ongoing firehose of information. It's so difficult to have an opinion, or a point of view, that isn't immediately compromised by new information, another study, someone else's insights or fake news. Even self-help has become a form of surrendering our power to someone else's 'expertise.' What happens is that we end up doubting our own knowing or intuition.

Today's chapter is an invitation to switch off distractions, turn the volume down on the noise, release ourselves from Netflix binges, social media updates and the momentary flashes of dopamine we get with every like and retweet.

We are going to consciously choose silence, solitude and quality time with ourselves so we can sink inwards and deep-wards to begin to listen to the sounds of our soul's whispers. We commit to stop spreading ourselves thin, and rather to sinking deeply inwards. To curl inside ourselves like a sea creature in its shell. It is what John Keats, the poet, called 'the cave of quietude.'

We have to get away from the noise. To do so, we need time alone. We need silence.

In order to see birds, it is necessary to become part of the silence.
ROBERT LYND

Alone and in silence, we inhabit the shape we truly are. Inside you is a rich life waiting for you to discover it. There is no plus-one for this party. It's a solo gig.

I woke up to this in my early twenties when I realized that though I was expected to love live concerts and clubs, I detested them. For a long time I pretended to enjoy excursions into these smoky, noisy venues because I wanted to fit in. I dragged myself to disco-ball, epilepsy-inducing, light-flickering, eardrum-damaging clubs, drank alcohol I didn't want, and tried to be sexy on the dancefloor. I invariably came home with terrible stomach cramps. One day, I just knew that I couldn't do it anymore. And so, I stopped. I felt my spirit chiropractically align. I became myself.

Here's a poem I wrote about the first night I moved into my own apartment in a suburb in Johannesburg called Yeoville. I was 25.

Yeoville, first night

That first night
in Yeoville
I lay in my bed
and called the ceiling, mine
the walls, 'dearly beloved,'
the outside noise of motorbikes
and alcohol,
'friend.'

I think
I knew then
that aloneness
was the key
to becoming;
I felt how everything
had been a delay,
a long wait
to begin – this – this
quiet curiosity;

that in my own space
I'd soften
open the folds
I'd tucked tightly in,
find 'her,' that
unaccompanied girl
a stowaway til now.

> I pulled back the curtains
> to let the moon in,
> and leaned on the night's shoulder
> and I told the truth
> for the first time.

To truly know ourselves, we have to reach within, go deeper than the noise, into the under-voice, the voice beneath the voices. Here, we discover our uniqueness. It has an edgy quality to it; it's mysterious and strange, even to us. It is where we harvest insights, perceptions and intuition.

Our desire to belong to a part of ourselves is great and cavernous.

Joseph Campbell said in the Hero's Journey: 'you have to learn to recognize your own depths.'

We make commitments to be faithful and loving to others, but we forget to make those vows to ourselves too.

To make these commitments, we need to go alone, and we need to go far. Further than we can go when we're in the company of others.

Aloneness, and the quality of silence it opens to us, is like a secret doorway into our depths.

It's not only introverts who need this. We all do.

To know what we think, we need to know who we are – who we really are when no-one's looking and we are free of others' expectations.

Alone, maybe you find that you sing. Talk aloud to the cats and the pot plants. Are a contented nudist. A gifted pasta maker. Fantasize about other paths you might have taken. These are your secret selves.

In solitude, we resuscitate our dreams, ask the hard questions, interrogate our choices, plan our escape, cry over spilt milk, wish for more, ask forgiveness, break our vows, figure it out, make it work, and slowly remember what life is asking of us.

We breathe into the forgotten chambers of our being… put a brush to canvas… look at ourselves in the mirror and say, 'Sweetheart, it will be okay'… dream of what else there might have been. Alone, we never ever apologize. For any of it.

In this space, we begin to ask that flickering endless inquiry: Who am I?

Maybe this is where we show up as our truest selves.

AFFIRMATION

Go alone and go deep.

WRITING SKILL

I want to teach you list-making.

We all know how to make lists, but they're mostly to-do lists. This is a very different kind of list.

Lists are how we brainstorm around a particular idea, and they have this generous quality of being self-generating because they act like a prompt to your brain.

So let's say you have a list such as:

- All the things I love – you might start with ten things on that list, but every day, you will add to that list because you've subconsciously sent your brain on a treasure hunt, and your brain will quietly go away and collect more things to add.

These lists can spawn overnight – they are hugely fertile because you're listening internally.

The reward for your listening will be in what you hear.
RUMI

Our hearts and souls are constantly speaking to us, in whispers – they never yell at us. Which is why the silence and quiet are companions to this state. And in this silence, in the list-making enterprise, you will hear yourself, you will come to know yourself, you will feel the fertility of your creative mind at work.

e e cummings writes that being ourselves in a world that is trying constantly to make us like everyone else is a lifelong battle we each have to fight and keep fighting.

WRITING EXERCISE

Make a list. Pick any topic.
   If you need help, try any one of these:
   - The things I am brilliant at
   - The people I forgot to thank
   - The happiest moments of my life
   - A list of all the lists I want to make

Once you start, you will overflow with abundance.

REFLECTION QUESTION

I can access my own depths best:

- *when I am in nature*
- *late at night when everyone is asleep*
- *when I meditate*
- *when I listen to music.*

NOTES

Chapter 3
JUST BELIEVE

When we write, we are learning to trust ourselves in a very particular way.

Writing is an act of creation – and we are all, unconsciously, involuntarily even, a repository of an infinite potential for creation. I hope you got some sense of that from the list-making exercise.

We have an infinite ability to create, but many of us don't. Or we start and we get stuck. What happens?

We stumble when we suffer from a failure of self-belief.

We have no faith or conviction in our ability or in the value of what we're doing.

These little infections contaminate us: 'Who'm I to write? Why should I do this? I can't. I have nothing to say.'

My heart can break over and over again when I mentor people who do not believe in themselves.

This lack of self-belief is like a virus we pick up in our nurturing environments, often in our early years, due to events or situations in our families of origin, or our encounters with education system. What happens is that our blossoming sense of creativity is starved, stamped on and often, gravely damaged.

And we don't even realize it.

A failure of self-belief shows up for us as adults in all kinds of ways including self-doubt, worrying about what others think of or say about us, low self-worth or poor self-esteem, feeling we are not enough, desperation for approval, waiting for permission, perfectionism, indecisiveness, fear of being judged, not wanting to rock the boat, always wanting to keep one's options open, not being able to choose between options, not trusting our own instincts.

It can also show up in self-sabotaging actions, vagueness, a lack of clarity or direction, narcissism, avoiding anything unless one can do it perfectly the first time, being overly self-critical, being overly loud or painfully shy, holding back, hesitating, reluctance to speak one's mind, paralysis or stagnation due to fear of making the wrong decision, hypervigilance to one's own needs or other peoples' needs, always compromising to keep the peace, fear of not being liked or desperation to be popular, attention-seeking behaviours, gossiping or speaking negatively about people behind their backs, always needing to ask other people's opinions before one can make up one's own mind, procrastination and a lack of clarity on what one's own values and beliefs are.

When we are easily manipulable, and suggestible, it may be that we are shrinking from our own sense of what we want or need in our own lives.

When we don't know what matters to us and what's worth fighting for, when we don't do what we say we're going to do and we don't take ourselves seriously, then we are suffering from a failure of self-belief.

Now if you recognize yourself here – as I think we all do in some way – can you, instead of hardening into judgement or blistering into criticism, soften into self-compassion and see the exquisite vulnerable humanity of your soul?

Can we honour that these behaviours are survival tools we developed from our early years? Maybe they are the result of experiences such as learning difficulties at school, neurodiversity that was undiagnosed, identity issues, being part of a marginalized group, trauma of any kind, being forced into roles like having to be a parent to our own parents, addictions, never having had our preferences, dreams or wishes seen or respected, and past failures that haunt us.

When it comes to writing, our failure of self-belief can show up as never fully owning our desire to write. We keep it as a hobby because that is where it is safe. We might underplay how much we love writing or how important it is to us.

We may feel ashamed of our desire to write and believe we're not up to it. We might romanticize the writing life or believe we have no talent, and so we make excuses about why we can't or haven't started writing yet.

We may struggle to make any kinds of decisions including where we start, what story we begin with, and we certainly will stumble around structural narrative decisions.

I've even mentored writers who get stuck on a name for their main character and believe they cannot move forward until they have the perfect name. So they stay mired in that place, hoping that at some point, the perfect name will come to them and that's going to be the magic key that will unlock their writing life and their writing career.

Another symptom of a failure of self-belief is writers' block that becomes entrenched and we cannot move past.

This distrust of self becomes a creative stutter.

 ## AFFIRMATION
Yes, I can.

WRITING SKILL

Failure of self-belief can show up in someone's writing as an overuse, or default into the passive voice.

Just a quick refresher: an active sentence has a subject, a verb and object:

'I wrote a book.'

The passive voice would read: 'The book was written by me,' or just, 'The book was written.' Sometimes the subject is swallowed up and disappears in the passive voice.

This can signal a consciousness that wants to bypass the agency that language and writing asks of us.

Strong writing (writing that at its core is claiming, 'Hineni') usually has a subject, verb and an object. One sentence follows another, moving us ever forward in the action or emotional arc of the story.

If we are the subject of our writing but we use the passive voice, by implication, we are swallowed into the action and occluded. We become invisible. Or more accurately, we are making ourselves invisible.

So instead of, 'I moved out,' we might write, 'The move was made.' Where is the 'I' in that sentence? It's gotten lost.

So our writing often gives us clues about our consciousness and what is happening for us at a soul level.

Writing is a powerful, energetic tool when it has pace, direction and it flows.

When it does that, it helps us move through experiences and

process emotions rather than get entangled in memories. It has the energetic strength to manoeuvre us like a tide or the current of a river and carry us from one sentence to the next, from one scene to the next, from one emotion to the next.

Writing begins with saying *yes*. It is an affirmation of your longing to write and your intention to do so.

I invite you to say yes to your writing.

Invite it in without expectation. Go on a blind date with it and see where you end up.

> *The worst enemy to creativity is self-doubt.*
> **SYLVIA PLATH**

Conviction is the foundation of your writing voice. It cannot be found externally, and once we hold it energetically, it becomes a guardian of the creative process. It cannot be any other way. For if we don't fundamentally believe we have something worth saying, it doesn't matter how much of the craft we learn. We'll never put anything we've written out there. Because we will always hold ourselves back with the thought: *what will people say and think?*

The other day I was watching a spider going about its spiderly business, spinning a web. I thought to myself, just look at that little creature – it doesn't stand back and ask itself, 'I wonder if I should spin a web here, or wait, maybe over there is a better spot. But what about that window… or the tree outside…'

It doesn't second guess itself or get tied up in self-doubt. It just goes about its business.

So let's be more like spiders. Ask yourself – what would a spider do?

Let's not hijack ourselves by getting caught up in a complex matrix of self-limiting ideas and beliefs, including our need to be perfect.

The greatest strength we develop in the creative life is self-trust.

One of my favourite quotes by the poet Robert Frost hangs above my desk, which reminds me that we are always believing 'ahead of our evidence.' He asks what evidence he had that he could write a poem – all he had was the belief that he could. Believing in something, he says, is the most creative impulse in each of us.

Frost is saying that believing in yourself is a choice. It's up to you. Self-belief is not a fact – it's an attitude – and we measure it based not on who we are, but on what we do.

Believing in ourselves is a way of taking ourselves and our lives seriously – not casually. We make our lives sacred, and we honour our humanity when we take ourselves seriously.

Use the active voice unless you are consciously using the passive voice. The passive voice should always be a choice you make because it enhances your meaning.

'I ate ice-cream' vs 'Ice-cream was eaten.'

'I made the bed' vs 'The bed was made.'

'I am singing' vs 'The song is sung.'

'We asked them to send help' vs 'They were asked to send help.'

Do you feel the difference between the active and passive sentences? Can you say what that feeling is?

WRITING EXERCISE

'I am here to say yes to…'

REFLECTION QUESTION

How does conviction show up in your life?
- *I can be self-compassionate when I make a mistake or don't get it right*
- *I can recognize and manage my self-sabotaging behaviours*
- *I don't have to be 'good' at something to enjoy it*
- *I feel joy rather than jealousy of the success and happiness of others.*

NOTES

Chapter 4
NURTURE WHAT'S HERE NOW

In the poem 'Lost' by David Wagoner in which a child is lost in a forest and asks an elder how to find her way home, he writes that where we are is called 'here' and we must treat it as a powerful stranger. The 'hereness' of wherever we are calls us to know and be known.

Take a moment to look around you.

Wherever you are is what we call *here*.

Here.

This moment, this space in which you inhabit this moment. Here.

But for many of us, here and now is the hardest place to stay. In fact, we will do anything to be anywhere else but here.

I sometimes think we humans have a design flaw.

Why do we find it so hard to just be where we are?

We spend so much time dislocating ourselves from the moment by reaching backwards and arching forwards, ruminating, anticipating, regretting, hoping.

We can be tragically nostalgic. And I am really talking from personal experience.

Whenever I travel from Australia back to South Africa to see my parents, as soon as I step out of the taxi, my dad folds me into his arms, bursts into tears and sobs, 'But you're only here for three weeks.'

My poor dad. As soon as I am right there, he is already anticipating me being gone. Every time he looks at me, he looks with eyes that are already missing me.

He cannot just be in the moment with me without anticipating the loss of when I will leave again.

We all do this. We all nurture a sense of foreboding of the way the future is going to rob us of the moment we're in.

Tennyson described us humans as 'the intense atom.'

In my favourite Leonard Cohen song, 'Come Healing,' he refers to us as 'troubled dust.' We fret. We worry, we anticipate, we fantasize. We are a species that agonizes, analyses, overthinks.

Because of our tendency to live up in our heads, we can get easily scattered and splattered in trawling back to things that have happened and anticipating things that have not yet transpired.

We obsess about what is long over. We get laden with regret. We self-flagellate over our mistakes. We project and fantasize into the unknown future, struggling to be right where we are – in the present moment. Do you ever have that experience where you obsess over a moment – thinking of the perfect comeback, what you should have said, could have said, wish you'd said.

We radiate our life's energy backwards – wishing things hadn't happened as they did; and forwards, expending anxiety about what has not yet happened.

So much of our suffering is right here in this trawling of the past and throwing nets out into our future. I am particularly prone to the anxious part – thinking about the future. Overplanning it.

I love this quote by Robert Downey Jr who said, 'Worrying is like praying for things you don't want.'

So our challenge is to stay in the moment that is right here. And to pay attention to what is right in front of us.

It's a fullness of presence, a refusal to be tempted out of the moment that sits curled up in our laps like a contented cat.

There is a story about the Buddha – after he attained enlightenment under the Bodhi tree, he got up and walked amongst ordinary people with this blissful smile on his face. People kept asking, 'What are you? Are you a man? Are you a god?' And all he said is, '*I am awake.*'

Being in the present moment is about that sense of wakefulness, alertness to what is around you. If you've ever given a child your full attention, you'll know that you have to get onto your knees, lock eyes with them at their eye-level, abandon your distractions and offer your whole self to them.

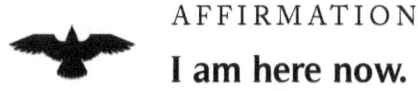

AFFIRMATION
I am here now.

The beauty about giving this kind of full, unadulterated attention is that we illuminate whatever we touch with this attention. When we stay in the moment, we are able to hold something briefly in our hands and pay a certain quality of attention; and in doing so, we make it sacred.

We focus, and in focusing, we honour the object or subject of our focus. By the act of being with what is by its nature passing, we acknowledge the impermanence of the moment, knowing that as we attend to its presence, it is fading, but can we do it without lapsing into pre-emptive nostalgia.

This is what it means to make each moment count.

When my cat Tanaka was diagnosed with kidney disease, I knew her time was limited, and I was able to bring a certain focus to our relationship. I watched her so closely, I listened to her purr and little meow, and I wrote everything so that I wouldn't forget anything about her. The piece I wrote about her ends with this:

> Now at night, I lie with her beside me, a raggedy parcel of cat-bones and fur, my heart bursting. 'At most, a year,' were the vet's words. But with so little appetite, I wonder. I have never nursed a dying person. My time will come. But here I am, loving what is leaving me. It is a painful, exquisite gift. I am in presence with impermanence and the fragility of life and friendship and unconditional love. I rest my head beside her and tell her the story of our friendship. She musters a meow, without sound. She purrs into my hand. She knows me so well. I don't want her to go. And I am filled with tender gratitude.

Writing is one way we can practice and get better at becoming a creature of the moment.

Writing is a way of us making space for awe.

We engage a sense of, 'Wow, look where I am. Look what's here right in front of me.' Our attention becomes a lantern, a spotlight, a ray of sunshine.

When we give our own lives this kind of attention, they too become illuminated. Illumination transforms the ordinary into the sacred.

So dear friend, can you bring this kind of attention to yourself?

Can you record the quiet miracles around you?

What greets you each moment?

Can you see your world through unaccustomed eyes?

When you drive past a meadow, do you exclaim, 'Look, cows'?

When you see a rainbow, are you startled into breathlessness?

When a whale or dolphin breaches, the moon is full outside your window, a kookaburra calls, can you see these as invitations to just be here now?

The generosity of this practice is that when we write into the sensations and feelings of the present moment, we encase it in the resin of language. And it becomes a moment we get to 'keep.'

Staying in the present moment also helps us build stamina for staying with difficult things. Life will deliver experiences that are complex, uncertain, doomed, filled with ambivalence and ambiguity, disillusionment, tragedy, pain, impending grief. The work is to stay in that space without becoming frustrated, overwhelmed, frozen or distracted.

To simply be here now.

WRITING SKILL

Let's think about tenses.

Look at these three sentences:

'I love him.'

'I loved him.'

'I had loved him.'

A tense change causes a shift in nuance and changes the way we feel and where we are situated.

'I love him' is the story of a love in flow – the highpoint of a heart's journey. We are in the immediacy of love. We are close-up, a confidante. When a writer uses the present tense, it's an act of intimacy.

'I loved him' is almost the opposite. Perhaps it's a story of regret, a betrayal, a loss. We have loved and lost. That tense change is a keynote of sorrow. 'I loved him… but I don't love him anymore.'

We choose to use the past tense when we are standing a distance away from the action, when a chapter is closed.

'I had loved him' has a fancy grammatical name – the past perfect tense. It tells us that the loving was done in the past, before something else happened.

'I had (already) loved him when I realized he didn't love me back.'

First, I loved him. Then something else happened… I stopped loving him. He left me. I ran away with his best friend.

Our tenses are part of the meaning we create when we write.

They mark where we are standing in the telling. Inside the moment or outside? Close or far?

Language positions us, not just as a matter of syntax and comprehension, but emotionally. It's the angle of the light when the camera goes *click*. Tenses tell us more than where in time things took place. They speak of closure or endless longing. They measure our proximity. They are lenses.

WRITING EXERCISE

Look around you. Where are you?

Write a paragraph in the present tense about where you are here now. So you can begin with the prompt, 'Right now, I am…'

Once you've finished writing, write the same paragraph in the past tense.

Notice what difference a tense makes.

REFLECTION QUESTION

The most accessible way for me to be present in the moment is by:
- *being in my body*
- *journaling*
- *focusing on my breath*
- *updating my Facebook status.*

NOTES

Chapter 5

BREATHE, BATHE, BAKE BREAD

The last chapter was about how to stay in the present moment.

One of the most accessible ways to do this is to sink into and then stay in our bodies.

We spend a lot of time trying to escape from them.

There's a famous line in *Dubliners*, written by James Joyce, in which he writes that Mr. Duffy 'lived a short distance from his body.'

That might describe any one of us on a bad hair day. Or when we have a stomachache, hangover or sore throat.

We are trapped in our skins – we can't escape our bodies until we die – but we can treat them like a distracted parent who pays scant attention to a toddler crying to be noticed.

We can be brutal towards our own flesh: we don't get enough rest; we push ourselves beyond our stress limits; we dull our senses with sugar, salt, caffeine, alcohol, noise, drugs, games, screens.

There's an advert on television for a headache tablet. It shows people leading busy lives as teachers, entrepreneurs, athletes; and the selling point is, 'We're too busy for headache, period pains,' – this drug is for busy people who don't have time to be sick.

This advert always strikes terror in my heart – the idea that we must override pain, exhaustion, hay fever, just so we can get back to our super important agendas.

Those super important agendas keep us out of our bodies and in our heads.

But in this chapter, I'm advocating on behalf of the body.

We all need a break from our heads where the chatter is, where the inner critic governs like a dictator. Between our ears is the kingdom of self-judgement.

What we want is to take a little excursion into the countryside of corporeality. So we can tune into the silence of sinew, the music of muscle, the beat of blood.

This chapter is a chance for you to sink down below your chin.

To loosen yourself from analysis, over-thinking, rationalizing, reminiscing, planning so that you can hear:
- the beating of bones and blood,
- the tales in your tissues,
- the voices of your valves,
- the accents of your alveoli.

We want to breathe, bathe and bake bread.

Can we slip into our bodies the way we might slip into a body of water? Can we experience the full sensual experience of hunger, pain, exhaustion, lust – the whole glorious cacophony of our senses?

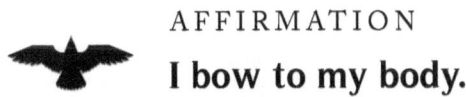

AFFIRMATION
I bow to my body.

Go and google e e cummings' poem, 'i like my body when it is with your body.'

Read it aloud.

Isn't it a luscious, delicious celebration of the body? We often only experience how much we love our bodies when our bodies are with another body, and we are being made love to or making love. But we can make love to ourselves when we stay in our own bodies.

But being in our bodies can be very painful too. We may not feel safe to be in our bodies because of past trauma. Or maybe our body is keeping a secret we are not ready to share or even to know. Or perhaps we don't like our bodies because we've internalized the idea that there is something bad or wrong about them. I invite you to simply notice what comes up for you when you are in your body – that's all.

At different times, our bodies may feel like completely different creatures. At times, we feel we belong inside them. At times, we feel betrayed and let down. Sometimes we feel like strangers in our own skin.

Our bodies reveal our histories, hold our pain and keep us company through our lives.

We can experience our bodies as:
- home – a place that is safe and nurturing,
- a place of exile – when we feel unwell or in pain,
- a witness,
- a memory keeper,
- a storyteller,
- an oracle,
- a guide / teacher,
- a map,
- an enemy / traitor.

Take a moment now to sink into your body.

Breathe as deep as you can.

As you sink into your body, only go as far as you feel able to go. Maybe you'll go just below your chin, into your throat. Maybe you can melt a little lower into your ribcage. Just go as far as you can. Let your breath be your guide.

If you feel stronger and able to go further, keep going.

Plunge further down into the belly.

Take a few deep breaths as you take that long, slow elevator from the penthouse of the brain, deep down into the chambers of your body. Get off on whatever floor is the right one for you.

How does it feel to be in your body right now?

Are you in any pain?

Are you hot? Cold? Just right?

Can you feel the rumblings of hunger? Thirst?

Are you comfortable?

Are you clenching any part of your body?

Just notice. Use your senses.

Our senses are doorways into deepening our presence.

Though we all have a number of senses, some of us more than others, each of us sees, hears, smells, tastes and touches in a slightly different way, in ways that are unique to us.

Let's take seeing. Some of us see colors; others see shapes. Some of us notice the spaces around things more than the things themselves. Some of us hear through sounds, some of us hear undertones and some can hear the silences.

And as we stay with a sense, and deepen into it, we begin to experience the object our sense rests on in a more complex way.

Gustave Flaubert wrote, 'Anything becomes interesting if you look at it long enough.'

When we look, do we really see things? Or do we gloss

over, glance? Pausing is a way of slowing down our sensual experiences.

Remember what Rafiki tells Simba in *The Lion King* when Simba looks in the water and says, 'That's just my reflection.'

He says, 'Look harder.'

And then Simba sees his father.

Can you find ways of seeing, hearing, tasting, touching and feeling that are new?

Can you see what is invisible or hidden?

Listen for what you haven't yet heard – the undertones, subtexts?

Can you taste the base notes of what you put in your mouth?

Come curiously, without assuming you know what you will find.

Every morning when I go for a swim in the ocean, there isn't a single day when the beach is the same as it was the day before. Whether it's the swell, or the seaweed washed up, or the light on the water, the bluebottles dotting the shore break. Same beach, but every day it is a new sea. And I love its kaleidoscopic personalities.

The poet Mary Oliver writes that she looks every moment of every day – she is never finished with looking. And what she means is not just hanging around but being somewhere as 'though with your arms open.'

Whatever we see, smell, taste, touch or hear will remind us of something particular from our own memory bank; and these unique associations seep into our sense of things and make them new.

Can you experiment with slowing down your physical experience? Try eating more slowly. Watching more closely. Moving weirdly. Touching something in an unusual way.

Wearing a piece of clothing inside out. Listening to what is not being said, or to the silences around things.

WRITING SKILL

Synesthesia is when we use a description of one kind of sensation to describe another. We give sounds colours, we attribute sounds to smells, we give smells a texture. Here are some examples:
- the whisper of clouds,
- the siren of his gaze,
- the darkness – a symphony of shadows,
- the velvet of the vanilla cream,
- a pop of yellow,
- the grain of her laughter.

WRITING EXERCISE

Write about the most intense physical pleasure you've ever experienced and/or the worst pain you've ever felt. Can you use all five of your senses to describe it – sounds like, tastes like, smells like, looks like, feels like; and then use synesthesia to make it fun? (I would probably write about swimming in the ocean and coming across a blue groper right under my nose. Instead of describing it as *cobalt* blue, I'll write, 'It swims past me, a *trumpet* of blue,' – using a sound word to describe a colour).

REFLECTION QUESTION

How does sinking into your body make you feel?
- *I don't like being in my body*
- *I feel kinder and more compassionate to it*
- *I feel more grounded*
- *It accentuates where my body hurts.*

NOTES

Chapter 6
GIVE IT A NAME

Have you ever felt a mess of sensations and emotions without being able to pinpoint what you're feeling?

My late grandfather Solomon wrote about such a moment in his memoir, *Shalechet*. It was the early 1920s in Kovno, in Eastern Europe, and he was learning to become a printer. He had already survived smallpox and other serious ailments. Oh, and he had just met my grandmother.

He writes:

> I had no permanent employment… My nerves were on edge. At times I felt that something was wrong with my health. I felt the symptoms of (various ailments) mentioned in medical lectures.
>
> Because of working conditions, the printing trade was considered a health hazard. More often than not the premises were situated in a cellar… which was damp in winter. The type caused lead-dust to form and many printers were adversely affected by this. I thought I was becoming a candidate for tuberculosis. On the quiet, I went to see a doctor and told him of the pain in my chest. After a thorough examination, x-ray (not a very common procedure in those days),

and a book of injections the doctor discovered that I was in love.

How often have we felt a nameless, shapeless feeling inside us, and finally when it is named, the formless fog is siphoned back into a lamp like an escaped genie?

When something has a name, it has a shape. We know how to situate ourselves in relation to it.

A nameless disquiet becomes 'anxiety.'

A low grade feeling of exhaustion has a label – 'depression.'

The chaos settles – naming is a diagnosis. A verdict.

It restores order to the world.

Ah, that's what it is.

'This surveillance of my whereabouts is coercive control.'

'This undermining is gaslighting.'

'This emptiness is grief.'

'This loneliness is autism.'

The moment we have a name, our relationship to an experience shifts.

We feel more grounded.

We can orient ourselves in relation to the experience.

We might be able to take right action because we know what we're dealing with.

So naming is a vector. We can get our bearings in relation to something when it has a name.

My novel, *Things Without a Name*, begins like this:

> Nonna taught me how to read. My first book was made of cardboard and had pictures with words next to them. Nonna pointed at the letters next to

a picture of a house. H-OU-Z. She pointed at the letters alongside a bird. B-I-R-T. Because she has a thick Italian accent, I learned to read English with an Italian accent. "NONNA—is me. FAITH—is you. Everywhere you look, up, down, here, there, things have a name."

"Why must things have names?" I asked.

"Otherwise how must we know what it is? Things need names for onderstanding. So if you ask for *fiore*, a flower, I don't bring you *ragno*, a spider." And she wiggled her nine fingers like a spider's legs.

"But I like spiders," I told Nonna.

"Yes, but a spider is not a flower."

"What about things that don't have names?" I asked. "Like the colour of yesterday and the things we forget."

Nonna lifted her four-fingered hand to her mouth like she was holding a truth from slipping out. She smiled briefly before she answered me:

"They don't exist. And if they do, they are *dimenticato*. Lost."

That book is about finding names for things inside ourselves so we can claim our power and love ourselves back into being.

Naming can also be restorative.

I have a story about my mother to share.

She was an only child. As a little girl, she was desperate for a sibling, but my grandmother kept having miscarriages. But then she finally fell pregnant and all seemed to be going well, but she tragically miscarried when she was six months pregnant. I once asked my gran about it, and she told me, 'I believe it was a boy.'

Many years later I was doing a family constellation session and relayed this to the practitioner, who then said something transformative to me, 'Can you bring your mother's brother into the room?'

Until then, I had not thought of my mother as having had a brother. I had always thought of her as an only child.

But she did have a brother. She just never got to meet him.

This naming awoke such sorrow and compassion in me, naming this lost son and brother and child. My uncle.

Naming things can be restorative. It returns things to their rightful place. It plugs a hole that until that moment, we may not even have known was there.

When we write into our experiences, and we identify and label the experiences, we give them names: neglect, grief, ambiguous loss, abandonment. And in doing so, we really get to witness it. It's as if the experience has been waiting inside us all this time, just needing to be seen, to be recognized, to be named. Once it hears its name, it can rest.

A coherence, a congruence, is restored.

Naming also has another quality. It can be like casting a spell – it can call something into being – which is why we must be careful about what we say about ourselves.

When my grandfather Solomon was a young boy, he got smallpox and was on the brink of death. His father Yitzchak Abba went to synagogue and renamed him Chaim, which in Hebrew means, 'life.' Who knows how these things work, but he lived.

***

Dave Eggers wrote a wonderful short story called, 'On Making Someone a Good Man by Calling Him a Good Man.' In which, Stuart doesn't like Phillipe, his friend Margaret's husband, because he's lazy and doesn't treat Margaret well. But one day Stuart witnesses Phillipe stopping a young boy from being bullied, and Stuart says to Phillipe, 'You are a good man.' And then, Phillipe's behaviour starts to change.

Eggers writes that though Phillipe never showed that he'd heard Stuart call him a good man, he started to become what he had been called. And Stuart began to think that perhaps each of us can be 'so easily improved' by what he calls this kind of 'semantic certainty.' He suggests that 'to be named is to be realized,' and that perhaps when something is confirmed in this way, we can drop the struggle of self-realization. We no longer need to guess or mistake ourselves for something we are not.

In the same way, when I'm feeling pretty ordinary and someone asks, 'How are you?' I say, 'I'm splendid.' And you know what, I always feel better, partly because it's impossible not to make people smile when you say the word *splendid*. And so, I become splendid.

AFFIRMATION

What I name, I become.

We name things to create a sense of order, but the trick is not to become attached to the label or to believe that once we have named something, that it can never be renamed or shake itself free of that label.

So we begin by finding the right word to attach to a feeling: this is happiness; this is regret, loneliness, abandonment.

Now let's expand this into a writing skill.

When we find words to hook onto feelings or experiences, we have made an excellent start.

But certain words can cover too much ground – words like love, happiness, abuse, justice, joy, sadness. They're too big, too broad. They are the country of a particular emotion. They are clichés.

When we say, 'I'm feeling sad,' it's like saying, 'I'm in Italy.'

It gives us an idea of the emotional location. But it doesn't show us exactly where we are.

Just like we all have fingerprints, at the same time, each one of us has unique shapes to our fingertips. And the same goes for our emotions. My sadness may approximate yours, they may overlap, but they are unique to each of us at the same time.

You'll often find when two people say, 'I love you,' to one another, that it's a mistake to assume they mean the same thing.

There are different languages of love, and people show love in different ways.

The writing skill I want to share is how we start with cliché and use it as a launchpad to go deeper.

When we are looking for language to fix to an emotion, let's begin with the word that covers too much ground – the cliché.

I invite you now to name the general territory that you are exploring. Is it happiness? Loneliness? Sorrow? Grief? Boredom?

Now see if you can narrow it down.

Your happiness, loneliness, sorrow, grief in any moment is a very particular kind of that emotion.

It mingles all your personal life experience with your

personality and your DNA and your thoughts, and your intergenerational history and where you are in your life and the time of day, your star sign and your microbiome – any other number of factors that you want to put into this cocktail.

So to simply call it by one name is to rob the experience of all that it could be or become.

Once you've designated the general territory, slowly inch forward one step at a time to nudge yourself into the particularities of that emotion until you can describe it with more complexity.

If you are feeling happiness, ask yourself what else is it tinged with?

Relief? Greed? Ego? Sadness? Does it overlap into any physical sensations? Does it come from a feeling of the satisfaction after a beautiful meal, so is it actually in fact, fullness? Does it have something to do with your thirst or hunger being met?

Does it have to do with the moon outside or the rain on your window, or the silky shawl of snow on your doorstep?

Is it a function of the weather?

Does it depend on the time of day?

The time of the month?

Is it linked to what's happening in your personal relationships?

Is it illuminated by the refracted glow of a goal you've just fulfilled? Of something you have lost?

As you can see, one emotion can take us anywhere and everywhere. It can be the doorway into the most complex and rich exploration of our internal worlds.

And it begins by naming.

WRITING EXERCISE

Find the emotional country you are in. Name it.

Now go deeper and see if you can describe the exact spot you're occupying there.

REFLECTION QUESTION

When I name an experience
- *I feel relieved to know I am not imagining things*
- *I feel more connected and empowered*
- *I don't feel so alone because others are experiencing similar feelings*
- *I don't feel that 'special.'*

NOTES

Chapter 7
SAVE TIME

> *I paint flowers so they will not die.*
> **FRIDA KAHLO**

One of the reasons we write is to hold on to the past. We want to keep records, to grasp what is fleeting, temporary, impermanent. To retain and reinvoke past experiences that otherwise would slip away into the stream of life. These are our treasured memories, the 'bright hawks of our life,' as Mary Oliver calls them.

Memory is the cornerstone of our conscious identities. Memory hold our stories. The stories of who we are and where we've come from.

Some of us are, by nature, archivists, historians, compulsively nostalgic and sentimental. We are the ones who keep detailed notes about life.

I have done this since I was fourteen and read *The Diary of Anne Frank* for the first time.

Not that my life was particularly interesting, but I recorded every moment, idea, insight, teenage crush, and thought that passed through my mind. It makes for cringeworthy reading now, when I read back through those diaries, but they are a fascinating insight into a teenage mind. I actually drew on some of my diary entries for a book I wrote on raising teenagers called *Love in the Time of Contempt*.

When each of my children was born, I began to write a diary for each of them to capture every moment of those precious years. I wrote down when they smiled for the first time; I recorded their first words, the funny things they said and did; and I gifted these diaries to them when they each turned eighteen. It was my way of saving time for them, by bottling all those moments in those diaries. It's a record of their childhood, and our relationship as mother and child. If I hadn't written them down, I would have forgotten them, and they would never know about them.

Pablo Neruda wrote, 'Life is so short, forgetting so long.'

Because life updates so quickly, we write to stem the tide of forgetting.

But even as we do this, memory is an imperfect storage tool. It crashes from time to time, it leaks, we lose some of our stories.

Memory is unreliable. It is situational – all tellings are coloured by who is telling the story; where that person is standing, their perspective, their values, their relationship to everything they observe. Ask the same five people who were sitting around a table what happened on a particular occasion – and you'll hear five different versions.

That doesn't mean anyone is lying – everyone is telling their version of what they remember. Prosecutors and defense lawyers in cross examination exploit this flawed nature of the human capacity to remember by making witnesses doubt themselves and by revealing inconsistencies in peoples' accounts of an event.

So memory is not a dependable vessel for enshrining facts

– but it does record feelings faithfully. When we 'remember something,' we are often remembering how we felt, and facts attach to the emotional valence of that moment rather than the other way around.

Sometimes we don't remember a particular time in our lives.

So does that moment become like a tree that falls in the forest when no-one is there to see it? Do our memories matter if we no longer remember them?

Sometimes what is more interesting about a memory is not what we remember, but what we forget.

How can we remember what we've forgotten?

I find this a fascinating question. We'll explore it in our writing exercise.

We may think we don't remember much about our childhood, or a particular event; but as soon as we start to write, doors begin to creak open. We catch a whiff of something, we hear a sound and we follow it, and we see where it leads us.

So how do we enter a memory? The trick is to do it through the doorway of our senses – find a smell, a sound, an image – this can transport us right back to a moment that we imagined was gone.

Our consciousness grabs onto this sensation, which in turn recruits others; and as they begin to thread together, this in turn sparks more details.

So we can recall lost stories.

Writing into a memory – even one we think we've forgotten – is one way to retrieve it.

I want to share with you two ways of thinking about time: chronological time known as Chronos, and transcendent time, called Kairos.

Chronos is linear and sequential. It is quantitative and

measurable, something we can spend and use up. It's a grid against which things happen. Time in this sense is passive and has no inherent meaning. It is marked only by its passing and our anxiety of it coming to an end, in other words, of death. It is how our ego perceives time.

There is a different way to think of time, and we call that Kairos. It is qualitative and is imbued with deep potential and meaning. There are moments in our lives that transcend chronological time, that seem imbued with destiny or creativity, a feeling of 'the divine order of things.' We're not worried about the moment ending or passing because it has a kind of eternal feeling about it. We were an active participant in its creation.

When we think about chronological time we might ask, 'What time is it?' or 'When does this start or finish?' or 'How long does this go on for'?

But when we think about it as Kairos, we ask, 'What kind of time is it?' 'What moment in time is this?'

It's the time of the soul, not the ego.

The difference is that chronological time happens to us, but we help co-create Kaironic time.

AFFIRMATION
Time doesn't just happen to me. I also leave my mark on time.

We all develop our own relationship with time, which becomes our history and memories. We carry these with us at all times, even if we don't consciously recognize that we do.

How is that possible?

Our reactions and responses to the world are the ways that history and memory show up for us in the present moment.

When I was no more than a baby, I had a few operations to fix tendon in my left hand after an accident. I have no conscious memory of the accident or the operations, but when I smell the antiseptic smell of a hospital, to this day, a visceral anxiety is triggered in me. I carry that history with me at all times.

All our responses to the world are clues to the way time has left its mark on us.

When we write to save time, we are actively and consciously remembering the past. We may want to preserve a moment, and never forget it. Or we may want to prevent someone we love from being forgotten so we write to capture them in time.

But friends, the most interesting paradox about writing is that as soon as we own our stories, the gesture of owning, naming, holding on, has this marvellous way of disentangling us – and we find, that in writing to hold on to something, we are able at last to let go of it.

This should bring some relief to your weary soul.

Our memories are never 'over' – they are never done and dusted. They live in us.

They have wired our synapses, they inform our choices, they give shape to our beliefs and values.

But in writing about the past, we can let it rest on the page. We can put it down.

WRITING SKILL

Think about how there are always multiple timelines in a story – the front story (what is happening now) and the backstory (what happened before).

Backstory is history or memory, and it always shows up in the front story to be confronted and somehow resolved. If we unpack that for ourselves, our wounds from the past show up in the present, and we get many opportunities in life to heal them.

WRITING EXERCISE

Start with the prompt:

'I remember...'

Allow yourself to slip back into a memory through the trapdoor of your senses and let yourself tumble backwards into a memory.

Once you've written for a while, switch to the prompt:

'I don't remember...'

Play with the idea of writing down what you can't remember.

REFLECTION QUESTION

I want to hold on to a memory to:
- *keep me connected to my history*
- *honour someone I love*
- *never forget the joy, pain and growth I've experienced*
- *celebrate that I survived.*

NOTES

Chapter 8
RELEASE

This chapter starts with a story about monkeys.

In southern Myanmar, monkeys are hunted for food.

Hunters set up traps made of hollowed out coconuts with holes the size of a monkey's paw. They fill the coconuts with peanuts or rice and then tie the coconuts to trees. Monkeys, lured by the smell coming from the coconuts, reach into the coconuts and grab a handful of rice or peanuts. But the opening is now too small for them to remove their fists. And so they stay trapped, their hands full of peanuts or rice, because they cannot let go.

Sometimes what we're holding on to is the very same thing that is trapping us.

We have to let go in order to be free.

In the previous chapter, I encouraged you to go back and remember things from the past.

In this chapter, it's going to sound very much like I'm contradicting myself.

When we are defined by a particular life experience, especially if it has been emotionally charged and traumatic, we develop an identity around that experience. We often get stuck there, caught in a story we cannot – or maybe don't want to release or relinquish. Maybe these old narratives serve us in some way – they provide safety, familiarity, a certain kind of attention that we need.

If we keep writing about the same story in the same way over and over again, it can retraumatize us. We can begin to obsess over the past and get caught in the loop of that story.

In order for us to not get caught in an identity that is entirely shaped by events from the past, we have to be able to both retrieve lost and missing pieces, and then let them go.

It doesn't benefit us to lug the trauma back into our lives and re-traumatize ourselves by replaying the trauma over and over and over again.

The intention that we set when we come to our own spiritual health must be to fully embrace all the events that have happened to us, but not to be defined by them.

Dr James Pennebaker, the founder of therapeutic writing, has used it to treat Post-Traumatic Stress Disorder (PTSD). His research shows how expressive writing aids the processing of emotion, overcoming trauma and emotional upheaval, resolving pain from the past, improving our health and building resilience.

It doesn't benefit us to write if it causes us to become unhealthily attached to our story or to an event. We write in order to become unattached. To let it rest on the page so we can turn and walk away from it. That is the gift that writing practice can offer us.

When my son was small and we used to walk along the beach, he would collect shells and pieces of glasses. But one day he said to me that by the time you get to the end of the beach, you realize that you didn't want it anymore.

I often think of writing in this way. We are trawling for these nuggets.

We want to find them, retrieve them and acknowledge them.

But maybe we don't want to take them home.

Maybe writing allows us to separate from the experience.

There it is, on the page.

We can identify a little less with it.

Writing is the process of taking something inside ourselves, externalising it, examining it with love, compassion and forgiveness, and then letting it be.

I'm not suggesting that we have to lose parts of ourselves in the writing. Or abandon them. Or walk away from them. Especially if abandonment and walking away is part of our trauma. But it is almost as if writing marks the place we have buried our ghosts, and we know we can come back and revisit and honour that experience, but we don't need to keep carrying it.

We don't need to remain attached.

This means unlearning a fundamental life skill.

We are hardwired for attachment.

From the moment we are born, we grab on to that first breath and from that second, we hold on to life. That becomes the way we operate. We hang on – to our bodies, relationships, a career, our identities, status, body image. We might hang on to a marriage, our children. We hang on to ideas, romantic fantasies about 'Someday, I will' and 'When this happens…'

We accumulate all these layers of attachment.

And this is the cause of much of our suffering.

Impermanence lies at the center of life, of everything.

Everything is temporary. How to release and let go is what we are here to learn.

In Buddhist practice, there is a meditation which goes, 'I am of the nature to get sick, I am of the nature to get old and I am of the nature to die.'

It is this consciousness of our own deletion, of the way in which we will be edited out of life at some point that allows us to come life with an absolute joy, a renewed sense of discovery, a sense of grace for every single moment that we have been given.

The defining moments of our lives are often those in which we have had to let go.

Come now, and let's release an experience so that we're not hoarding it, so that it isn't creating a blockade or blockage which accumulates like cholesterol in our spiritual arteries.

When we 'save a moment' by writing about it, we are shaking it free.

We're investigating how it is to when we write to unburden and empty ourselves.

Writing can cleanse us.

It can be like doing a spring clean or 'taking out the garbage.'

We make space and can move forward from memories and personal myths that have kept us trapped in their vice.

Let's think about writing as a practice of releasing, making space, and emptying.

I suspect that at the heart of all writing, we are all searching for a way to let go of something.

You know these Tibetan monks who create these exquisite sand mandalas. It is the most painstaking work, working with colored sand, and with such detail. When they have finished these sand mandalas, they then destroy them and they wash them away into the ocean. We can learn something from these sand mandalas – creation and a surrender of it back to the elements.

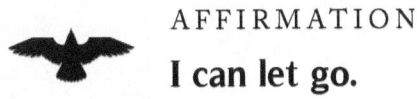

AFFIRMATION
I can let go.

WRITING SKILL

Let's look at deleting.

When we write, we often have to delete parts of what we've written. This is called editing, and I can tell you, writers generally don't like to let go of what we've written. We hang on to our darlings. We are attached to everything we've saved and put down on the page, and when we press the delete key on our computer and see our words vanish, we feel as if we are vanishing.

When we edit, we're afraid that we're losing something. It comes from a scarcity mentality because we hoard and hang on to what we have.

But here's another way to think about editing.

As soon as we take something away, we are adding space, we're making room for something other than words.

We can only really let go if we trust that there is more to come.

When we come from a place of scarcity, we hold on to everything, including every word.

So writing gives us a chance to practice not being attached to what we've written.

I have a friend who lost his mother very young, and because there were so many children and she was a single mother, he and his brothers and sisters were separated and dispersed amongst all the relatives. The only item that he inherited that belong to his mother was a fork.

Here is a poem I wrote for him about the story of this fork.

The Boy and A Fork

When a mother dies young,
her offspring are quickly
dispersed
no time for trawling
the treasures she may
have left behind.
A fork is all she left
on which to perch
his heart
and all the questions
her going brought with it.
He carried that fork with him
for twenty-three years
a three-pronged pedestal
in memory of
the touch of her lips.
At the age of thirty-three
he swam out into the mist
where the sea got dark
the tears of his ancestors
touched his skin
peeling the lostness
from his grasp.

He threw that fork
into the belly of the sea;
when he swam back to shore
he was, for the first time,
all alone inside himself
the burden of that steel
now the ocean's
and what he never had
gently sank
as he strode
across the sand
marking the earth
with his freedom.
What are you ready to let go of?

WRITING EXERCISE

This writing exercise is designed to show you how changing from the first, to the second, to the third person can help us to unhook ourselves from an experience.

First, write using first person, which is 'I…' and third person is 'she or he or they.'

I am pinned to my seat. Everyone's eyes are on me. I am hot with shame.

She is pinned to her seat. Everyone's eyes are on her. She is hot with shame.

A change of pronoun can create distance from an experience and help us to let it go.

Your writing prompt is:

I am ready to release…. (write for a while).

Then write about yourself in the third person, 'He / she is ready to release… (keep writing).'

REFLECTION QUESTION

Letting go makes me feel:
- *light and liberated*
- *afraid and needy*
- *unburdened*
- *ready for something new to take its place.*

NOTES

Chapter 9

BE A LOVER

Let's celebrate language now.

We can choose words to praise everything around us, and in so doing raise the vibration around us.

> *Sometimes you hear a voice through the door calling you, As a fish out of water hears the waves . . .*
> *Come back. Come back. This turning toward what you deeply love saves you.*
>
> **RUMI**

When I was fourteen, my father handed me a copy of Dylan Thomas's *Under Milkwood: A play for voices* and simply said, 'Read this.'

I remember a sensation tingling through my body as I read the opening paragraph which was filled with phrases like *'bible-black,'* and the *'sloeblack, slow, black, crowblack, fishingboat-bobbing sea.'* The words were chocolates in my mouth. I could taste 'the clip clop of horses on the sunhoneyed cobbles of the humming streets' on my tongue. A champagne of verbal bubbles.

As a child, I watched circus trapeze artists with bewildered fascination. I never once thought, *I wish I could do that*.

But when I read Dylan Thomas, I thought to myself, *I wish*

I could do that.

When we look back on our lives, we will find those places where love happened. We will remember how we trembled as light entered us, synapses mated, we felt the sizzle of the future entering us, as Rilke says, before it happened.

A professor of Shakespeare from my university days, with whom I correspond by email, once sent me his pepper soup recipe. Highlighted in huge red letters at the top of the recipe, he wrote: YOU HAVE TO LOVE THE VEGETABLES.

I think, if there is a secret to writing, it is: YOU HAVE TO LOVE THE WORDS.

Given that we're all born into a language that seeps into us by some magical neurological osmosis, perhaps we're prone to take for granted what we already possess. We have words. Having them, we don't think to love them. We're a species notorious for needing tragedy to illuminate our appreciation of what we already have, be it health, companionship, the most ordinary of happinesses.

I studied linguistics in my first year at university, and I vaguely recall decoding sentences to reveal deeply embedded structures, layers upon layers of parts of speech, quite algebraic and formulaic. Until then I never knew how innate composition is to language comprehension, and how invisibly interwoven structure is to meaning. It seemed like inheriting a genetic disposition for, say, classical music or drawing when others need years to learn the art. The talent is bundled into us, complete, awaiting discovery.

We can write flat, dull sentences. But we can write so that the words fill our hearts and swing us with giddy joy in the hammock of language. When we choose our words well, they jump up at us, lick our faces, feel soft and fleecy to the touch, prickly or viscous. Words dance in that part of our brains where imagination and language meet in secret rendezvous, in a hidden place we don't even know we're partying in. How can we not love words?

In *Beloved*, for which she won the 1993 Nobel Prize for Literature, Toni Morrison describes Paul D confronting Sethe with the atrocity of what she's done. He tells her, 'You got two legs, Sethe, not four.' And then, *'Right then, a forest sprang up between them, trackless and quiet.'*

Morrison writes with unbearable beauty that is spatial, sculptural. She makes her words places readers return to.

Terry Pratchett, the English author, instead of describing a dog as 'revolting and smelly,' describes it as 'halitosis with a wet nose.'

One sentence, like the opening line of Kafka's *Metamorphosis*, can open up a whole world:

> *As Gregor Samsa awoke one morning from uneasy dreams, he found himself transformed in his bed into a gigantic insect.*

Or the first line of George Orwell's *1984*:

> *It was a bright cold day in April and the clocks were striking thirteen.*

Writing encourages us to think, reflect, and nurture our own truths. Writing stretches our minds. It requires sustained concentration. This is good practice for life because everything worth doing takes time.

All great things in the world come from a patient unraveling of complex ideas – philosophy, politics, ethical morality.

Language supports us to refine our experience, solve moral conundrums, achieve social justice, and invigorate our hearts and minds. It makes us laugh and it makes us more soulful.

Words well-chosen shape our thinking and raise our standards. They give us nuance. They interject when we try to dumb ourselves down. They put love back into the world.

Writing makes us better people and helps us to love ourselves a little more.

But what does 'loving ourselves' mean?

Dropping self-judgment. Accepting our imperfections. And compassion.

All writing begins with self-compassion.

Writing is an act of dynamic empathy – for ourselves and for others.

We're often caught up in opinions, reproaches and criticisms. Our culture teaches us to analyze, disparage and bring others down to size. We ridicule people who make mistakes and vilify people on social media who disagree with us. Satire and some journalism are built on the impulse to demolish. This energy, as much as it is powerful and necessary in propaganda and in persuasive writing, is belittling and, at its core, arrogant. It is built on the idea of 'them' and 'us.' The subtext is, 'You are so stupid, and look how clever I am.' Its impulse is to destroy.

When we write, we're examining ourselves and our lives.

But those are the same eyes that silently judge: *I'm so fat. Are those new wrinkles? I wish I was prettier. I wish my teeth were straighter, my nose were smaller, my eyes less slanty…*

It's self-directed hate speech.

We need to come to our wounded places with a soft gaze and write about what we find difficult about being ourselves with great, gushing tenderness.

AFFIRMATION
I am here to love and be loved.

We teach the world how to love us by how well we love ourselves.

We cannot be believed if we claim we love others, if we do not know how to show that love to ourselves.

WRITING SKILL

Let's practice loving words in a way we haven't before.

Look at your use of adjectives and adverbs.

Adjectives are descriptions of nouns – the *big* boy, the *little* girl, the *beautiful* woman.

Adverbs are words that describe verbs. He ran *swiftly*; she shouted *loudly*. Those words – *loudly*, *swiftly* – are the adverbs. Often, you can lose those and rather find a better noun or a better description or a stronger adverb.

Instead of writing, 'He ran swiftly,' how about, 'He dashed,' or 'raced'?

'She shouted loudly' could become 'she yelled.'

Fewer words strengthen our writing.

Qualifiers like 'a bit,' 'like,' 'sort of,' 'somewhat' and 'quite' weigh down the writing.

Think about how you are putting two words together. If you are going to use an adverb or an adjective, see if you can slant it slightly paradoxically so that you create a little tension in the text.

A cold welcome.

A bitter smile.

A heartfelt indifference.

WRITING EXERCISE

Write a love letter to yourself. Praise what is brilliant, wonderful, fabulous and splendid about you.

Pay attention to every single word you use, especially your adjectives, adverbs and qualifiers.

Make it a powerful love anthem.

REFLECTION QUESTION

How do you show your love for your life?

- *acts of kindness to others and myself*
- *counting my blessings*
- *in movement and gesture — dancing, swimming, cooking, baking, creating*
- *devoting myself to my work.*

NOTES

Chapter 10
ASK QUESTIONS

*I have no special talents.
I am only passionately curious.*
EINSTEIN

The poet Rainer Maria Rilke wrote:

> Be patient toward all that is unsolved in your heart and try to love the questions themselves, like locked rooms and like books that are now written in a very foreign tongue. Do not now seek the answers, which cannot be given you because you would not be able to live them. And the point is, to live everything. Live the questions now. Perhaps you will then gradually, without noticing it, live along some distant day into the answer.

Sometimes we know a person we have just met could become a friend or lover simply by the questions they ask. Not by the opinions they hold.

Our creativity gets hampered in many ways – one of which

is the tendency towards binary thinking – right or wrong, left or right, black or white. Right and wrong is the language of opinions. And if our opinion is right, well, others must be wrong.

I am not a fan of opinions, I have very few, and I am looking for good homes for the ones I still have. I'm much more interested in people's stories, their interpretations, and the questions they have about life.

Fanaticism, extremism, orthodoxy, dictatorship – all share one thing in common – that there is one right way.

Religions and wars are fought because of this peculiar notion – there is only one right way and I know what it is.

We persecute people for their beliefs if they don't match our own.

But it is a dangerous place for us to build a spiritual life – any life, for that matter.

In all the great spiritual traditions, we honour the great unknown. At the heart of all great spiritual teachings is the idea of 'don't know.'

Curiosity and questions are the foundation of all growth and inquiry.

All breakthroughs in science, technology, medicine, the arts – come from dangerous questions.

- What if…?
- I wonder?
- Is that really true?
- What if it were not so?
- How else could we…?

A failure of curiosity can show up in our lives in some of these ways:

- judgement and criticism of ourselves and others,
- comparisons,
- thinking we're better or worse than others,
- envy and jealousy,
- making assumptions (both positive and negative),
- holding back from asking hard questions,
- doing the same thing over and over again,
- being moralistic,
- perfectionism,
- being a know-it-all,
- not listening when others talk,
- getting bored,
- taking things for granted,
- staying away from taboo topics,
- having fixed opinions,
- being unable to be with paradox or ambivalence,
- being afraid of not having answers,
- fear of change.

In order to break from these dulling states, we need to ask more and better questions, inquire and open ourselves to discovering something new, instead of predicting or predetermining what we might find. We want to clear the rust of prior judgement or fixed opinion. We can explore the world, armed with wonder, 'What will I find?'

We can never get bored if we come with a genuine sense of inquiry about our lives, what Buddhists call Beginner's Mind.

In the beginner's mind there are many possibilities,
but in the expert's there are few.
SHUNRYU SUZUKI

Curiosity is the hiatus between what we know and what we don't yet know.

It's that gap we always want to have. It's the space of possibility.

AFFIRMATION
Every door opens with what I don't know.

We can use writing to bring more curiosity into our lives.

Curiosity is a close relative of irreverence.

By its nature, it calls into question the sacred, pokes at dogma, provokes morality and tradition, and how things have always been done.

We don't just accept things 'because someone said so,' or 'because that's just the way it is.'

To be curious is to agitate.

When we are stubbornly curious, we might be called a stirrer, a maverick, a rebel. We may stray into disobedience, become disruptors.

This is one reason some of us are afraid to ask too many questions – we're nervous that it might get us in trouble, especially if we've been punished for this kind of behavior in the past.

But let's leave all that behind and wake up our curiosity without fear of repercussion.

Here are some prompts for you:
- Ask yourself: do I really love what I say I love? Do I really hate what I say I hate?
- Are my opinions really true? Are there times when they might not be true?
- Can I find some ambivalence in an experience I've always just labelled in a one-dimensional way? Can I find cracks in the beauty? Or beauty in ugliness? The goodness in evil or the perniciousness in the benevolent?
- When you hear something or read something and you find yourself agreeing or disagreeing, ask yourself why you agree or disagree? Are you practicing confirmation bias – does it confirm what you already think? What would happen if you decided to believe something that goes against what you already think?
- What would happen if I was wrong? If it were not so? What else is possible?

These are questions I love to ask myself because they halt my complacency, disturb my righteousness, loosen my convictions and let fresh air into the closed chamber of my understanding of the world.
- Look at something familiar again. Look deeper. What have you not noticed before?
- What do you wish you knew the answers to? What stops you from knowing these answers?

Any one of these questions, if pursued, might open your curiosity up. Just follow the thought or the emotion to wherever it may lead you. Don't try to work out where it's going – let it be a surprise. That's what you're practicing here – being surprised by your self.

WRITING SKILL

Let's notice and then question the clichés that show up in our writing.

Many of us think in clichés – hackneyed unoriginal, uninspiring thoughts that have been handed down to us:
- Marriage is a union between a man and a woman,
- Time heals all wounds,
- What goes around comes around,
- Every cloud has a silver lining.

When we write, we are aiming to avoid falling into clichéd expressions or thinking and question… is that really true?

If you feel yourself lapsing into clichéd, start there, and see if you can go deeper.

How to get out of cliché – ask: is it always true? Is it true for me? And what else? What am I not seeing? What other possibilities are there?

Churn it up.

Turn it over.

Poke it.

Question it.

Ask questions without looking for answers. Sometimes questions are just soul prompts.

Hang the questions like lanterns around you. What do they illuminate? What do they suggest?

WRITING EXERCISE

Make a list of all the questions that are unanswered in your life or that you wish you knew the answers to. Start with: I want to know why… Or I wonder why…

REFLECTION QUESTION

Curiosity shows up in my life as:
- *excitement at new adventures and opportunities*
- *interest in other people, especially those who are unlike me*
- *reluctance to stay in my comfort zone*
- *ease with chaos that seems to have no apparent order.*

NOTES

Chapter 11
CATCH A DREAM

All cultures and religions have ways of honouring our rich inner dream territory. Ancient Babylonians had professional dream interpreters – which is how Joseph in the Bible, by all accounts, survived. All indigenous cultures honour dreams in their own way with sacred scriptures, artefacts and rituals.

But it's only in more modern psychology that we really begin to understand the power of dreams.

Carl Jung in the prologue to his memoir *Prologue to Memories, Dreams, Reflections* wrote that the only events in his life worth telling were his inner experiences, which included his dreams.

He said, his travels, people he know and his surroundings had paled and faded – he couldn't recall these happenings. But his dreams were indelibly engraved on his memory; and writing about people, places and things he'd done seemed hollow and insubstantial compared to the light of inner happenings. He wrote that these were what made up the singularity of his life, and those were the substance of his memoir.

Dreams are the rich territory of our subconscious mind communicating to us through images, metaphor and symbolism. Dreaming is how we process our experiences, memories, thoughts and impressions. We access the invisible, mysterious aspects of ourselves through dreams.

Dreams can feel completely real. More real than real life.

The *Butterfly Dream* is one of two foundational texts of Taoism, in which Zhuangzi dreams he is a butterfly, and when he awoke, he did not know whether he was a man dreaming he was a butterfly, or whether he was a butterfly dreaming he was a man.

There was a time in my life when I was having such rich and wonderful dreams. I used to look forward the whole day to going to sleep again, just so I could re-enter those magical realms.

Dreams give us access to this part of ourselves we can struggle to find a way into – our subconscious, our deeper intelligence, our intuition.

What I love about dreams is that they don't make any sense – and we don't question that we might be sitting at a table with Wonder Woman, naked, about to launch a spaceship, and that our mother is knitting a blanket for us and counting napkins.

By writing down our dreams, we sometimes get answers to the questions we're struggling with in life.

Our dreams are part of our internal processing mechanism. By writing your dreams down, we're taking the subconscious and transitioning it to the conscious. And in this way, we're undertaking another layer of processing.

The reflection that we engage with in terms of symbolism helps us to make meaning. Dreams are windows into what haunts us, into our subconscious personality. They reveal our hidden selves – we get greater insight into ourselves. They shed light on our personal symbolism and the icons that speak to us

We might dream we are standing on a stage naked when we are about to start a new job. Or we dream a huge wave is about to crash on us when we're contemplating leaving a relationship. Or we dream we're herding sheep over a tricky mountain pass when we're about to have a new baby.

Dreams have been called the 'guardians of sanity' and allow us to heal. Research has shown that if people are stopped from dreaming, they can begin to show signs of mental illness.

AFFIRMATION

My dreams tell me who I am.

I've had a couple of predictive dreams – which unnerved me a bit. I once dreamt that branches were growing from my breasts – and a few days later I found out I was pregnant. I have sometimes dreamed things before they have happened. I only know this because I have recorded my dreams.

Rilke wrote, 'The future enters us long before it happens,' and I often think dreams are one way the future suggests itself to us if we know how to interpret them.

You can begin to see patterns emerging. If you have a recurring theme or symbol that keeps coming up, it could be a sign for you to look more deeply.

When we recall our dreams, we can become more creative in our thinking, because dreaming is uninhibited thinking.

Our dreams can become the source of creative projects. Apparently, Mary Shelley's *Frankenstein*'s monster came to her after an afternoon nap. Another dream-induced masterpiece is the Beatles song 'Yesterday.' Apparently, Paul McCartney woke up one day with the song playing in his head.

Our brains are like a computer running several different

programmes at once – and so our thoughts are unrestricted, unlike our programmed, conventional, restrictive conscious minds. We can make unusual associations between complex thoughts through our dreams and link ideas and thoughts that we wouldn't do consciously.

So how do we catch a dream in writing?

Our dreams take place inside our brains, and so when we think about writing them down, they have to undertake a journey and move from where they reside in the nest of grey matter in our heads, onto the page.

As you try to capture it, it seems to slip away.

Hélène Cixous writes, 'Dreams remind us that there is a treasure locked away somewhere and writing is the means to try and approach the treasure. And as we know, the treasure is in the searching, not the finding… To reach [this risky country where the treasure resides] you have to go through the back door of thought.'

Dreams are a snapshot of what is going on beneath the surface of our waking life, our habits, our obsessions.

Our dreams are how we come to know these hidden inner selves.

Jung wrote, 'No one who does not know himself can know others. And in each of us there is another whom we do not know. She or he speaks to us in dreams and tells us how differently she or he sees us from the way we see ourselves.'

Dreams can also be a doorway between the earthly and the spiritual realm.

They are a knocking from our subconscious to get the conscious mind to open a door and welcome something in.

We might have a dream that keeps coming back.

I became more curious and less casual about my dream life

when I recognized that they carry messages.

Not paying attention to them is like not emptying or opening an inbox or a mailbox and letting the messages pile up. We may miss an important invitation or piece of information.

And so it is with our emotional lives.

Guidelines for how to catch a dream:
- Record fragments – don't look for a storyline, what happened first, then what happened, just grab the impressions that remain;
- It doesn't have to make sense;
- Write it in the present tense:
- I am driving down a road, at dusk, and I am taking photos of mountains looming from the sea, that are in fact, huge succulents; and I am overwhelmed by their beauty. There are dark clouds on the horizon, and I know I cannot stop to look at them because a storm is coming. They are so utterly exquisite.
- Record the literal faithfully and allow space for the symbolic to emerge or suggest itself. You are looking to interpret or find an association – what the images in your dream remind you of;
- Don't rush to matchmake between the literal and the symbolic – allow the literal some breathing space;
- Each of us will have our own symbolic reference system. For example, water may have a specific association for you. If you grew up around a lake, it may represent your childhood. If you fell into water as a child or had some distress in a body of water, it could symbolize trauma;

- But often the images in our dreams have a poetic and mythic resonance that is larger than just your own experience – it could be universal. So water, for example, often represents emotion. And there are many dream dictionaries that will offer you some guidance on what things might mean. Don't take it all as gospel, only take what resonates for you.

WRITING SKILL

Let's explore one of my favourite writing tools – symbolism.

A symbol is something that stands for or represents something else. For example, a wedding ring symbolizes commitment. A puppy symbolizes hope. A bottle of champagne symbolizes celebration. It is the best way for writers to 'show' rather than tell. Symbols carry meaning for us – so we don't have to write, 'She was lonely.' We can simply show a single wineglass (which, by the way, can also symbolize joyous solitude). We don't have to write, 'He was grieving,' but rather show a wedding photo face-down, or dishes piled up in the sink.

In dreams, objects or people stand for bigger themes or issues in our lives. When we dream about an ex (whose heart we broke), or our father (who taught us how to play a musical instrument), these are aspects of ourselves. We can draw on both the universal or archetypal symbolism as well as our own, based on our personal histories.

For example, in my own symbolic library, mountains have a specific meaning. I once climbed Mount Mulanje in Malawi and struggled to get down after heavy rain. This was one of the first moments in my life when I thought I might die. If I dream of mountains, I am carrying that sense of foreboding. Traditionally, mountains symbolize working hard, overcoming obstacles, a spiritual quest or rising to heights.

When we're exploring symbolism – things mean what they mean to you. There is no fixed interpretation of what something means. When you've hit on the right interpretation, you'll feel it.

WRITING EXERCISE

Catch a dream in writing – last night's or one you've had a few times or just one that you remember.
- What images or people do you remember? Make a list.
- Now brainstorm or do a word association for what the image or person symbolizes (lightness, freedom, longing, what's missing in my life, etc.).
- Ask yourself, 'What else is this like? What does this remind me of?'
- Do some research to see if there is a universal resonance for this image.

REFLECTION QUESTION

My experience with my dreams is:
- *I don't remember them at all*
- *I don't think of them as significant*
- *I listen deeply to my dreams*
- *I've had dreams that have foreshadowed real life.*

NOTES

Chapter 12

STEER

An old couple are in a car – let's call them Harry and Mavis. Harry, who is at the wheel, shoots straight through a red light. Mavis clutches her bag nervously but she doesn't dare say anything. She doesn't want to be a backseat driver. Maybe Harry's eyes aren't so good anymore. But then, Harry shoots through a stop street. Still, Mavis doesn't want to upset him – he's very sensitive about being criticized. But when Harry takes a turn and drives the wrong way up a one-way street, Mavis can't contain herself any longer; and she says, 'Harry, my dear, what's the matter with you today? You've gone through a red light, a stop street and the wrong way up a one-way street.'

'Oh,' Harry replies. 'Am I driving?'

This jokes reminds me of my late Granny Bee, who was, may her soul be blessed, a truly terrible driver.

Many of us often find ourselves bewildered by the fact that we are, in fact, holding onto the steering wheel of our lives. Especially at times when we feel out of control. We may feel we're at the mercy of circumstance, other people, forces beyond our control.

Of course, there will always be situations we cannot change, predict or prevent. Events that ambush us.

Stock market crashes.

Accidents.

Unplanned and unexpected pregnancies and illnesses.

But sometimes – and only we can know when those times are – we attribute power to forces that, perhaps, are more within our sphere of influence than we believe.

In our writing, we are going to explore how and in what ways we can take personal responsibility for our lives.

Now there are some approaches to human existence which postulate that everything that shows up in our lives (including illnesses, bad luck, etc.) are the result of our choices – whether in this lifetime or others. If you adhere to the notions of karma or radical personal responsibility, you may choose to accept responsibility for everything that is in your life, simply because it is there.

Whether we believe this or not, what is certain is that we are responsible for:
- our choices,
- our beliefs,
- our values,
- what we tolerate,
- maybe not our emotions – but how we express them,
- how we teach others to treat us,
- our self-talk,
- our actions,
- our sense of self-belief,
- the meaning we give to situations,
- how we react to all circumstances,
- what we stay attached to and what we are prepared to let go of,
- what we focus on,

- what we regard as our business and not our business,
- how much we are prepared to be controlled by others (including institutions, rules and conventions, peoples' expectations, emotional manipulation by family members).

Sometimes we lapse into thinking other people make us happy, sad, angry, jealous. We regard them as the provocation for how we behave and react.

But friends, we know, don't we, that we are in control of how we react to others? Even when others behave badly towards us.

Please do not misunderstand me to be suggesting that we are to blame for what happens to us. There is a huge difference between taking responsibility (which is about taking back our power, affirming our reaction to a circumstance and taking action) and blaming ourselves, or anyone else (which is about feeling victimized by a circumstance, powerless, guilty, ashamed and often, paralysed about what to do).

Personal responsibility happens when we own our personal power. We determine what stories we tell about ourselves. We may choose to include in this contemplation of personal responsibility how we forgive those who have hurt us so that we are no longer energetically tied to them. The more we clean up our act, the less of our 'stuff' other people have to wade through to interact with us.

We maintain the hygiene of our emotional and psychic space.

How does personal responsibility show up in our lives?
- when we don't take things personally;
- when we take charge of emotional, financial and psychic energy leaks in our life;

- when we don't blame other people (or ourselves) for our circumstances;
- when we find effective actions and responses in which we maintain our power, voice and presence.

So how can we practice this in our writing?

As we put words on the page, we are engaging with our lives actively. We are investing energetically in an intimacy with ourselves.

We make choices about what we put on the page, what we leave out. We decide what meaning we are making of our experiences.

We are encouraged by the media to doubt our ability to make good decisions for ourselves – about what to eat, how to date, what to think of our bodies and how to be happy. Parents have so lost touch with their intuition that we read book after book on how to be decent parents, because we are certain we wouldn't know how to do it by ourselves.

Dr. Benjamin Spock's *Common Sense Book of Baby and Child Care*, first published in 1946, marked a break from the strict routines and discipline advocated by behaviorists who tended to enfeeble parents by labeling them ignorant. The opening lines of his book were simply, 'Trust yourself. You know more than you think you do.'

When we're not clear and don't trust ourselves, we can't help but make vague decisions. We 'leave our options open,' or we 'wait to see what will happen' or we 'go with the flow.'

When we do this, we splatter our focus and attention. We lose our power.

We are the only ones who can answer the question: *what gives my life meaning?* Not our parents, not our politicians, not our mates, our partners or spouses.

No-one else has the right answers to the questions in your heart.

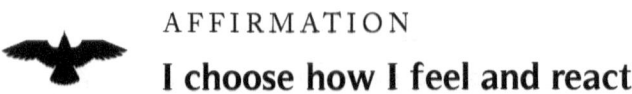
AFFIRMATION
I choose how I feel and react.

Many, many years ago, long before I was a published author, I wrote on a small card, 'I AM A WRITER.' I laminated it.

I tacked this card up on my computer screen with adhesive. Each day when I sat down to write, those words looked down on me.

An affirmation is an assertion, a verbal visualization, a pronouncement about a state of affairs. It steers our life in a particular direction.

When we assert in the present tense something we wish for in the future, we can begin to shape our reality.

I don't know enough about the sacred hidden geometries of intention and how they interact with destiny to say if this really is so. Did that card have any power? I know it got my head right. An affirmation is conviction in motion. It's the way we hold ourselves accountable to the longing inside us.

The affirmation made 'I AM A WRITER' true for me, in my heart. I was instructing the universe on the direction I wanted to steer my life in.

WRITING SKILL

Look at the word WRITE.

I want you to write it down: WRITE.

The letter 'I' is right in the middle of that word.

There is an 'I' in write.

When we write, we are asserting our agency.

When you write, remember, you are at the centre of whatever you're writing. How you see the world, how you experience it, your senses, emotions, memories, the meaning you make of it all.

Steer your narrative, hold onto the reins of whatever you're writing, and see when you tend to lapse into the passive voice, and how the 'I' disappears. In other words, where you give your power over to someone or something else. Then go back and rewrite it, using 'I,' and the active voice.

Goethe said, *'When you trust yourself, you will know how to live.'*

Trust yourself.

WRITING EXERCISE

Writing prompt: I am steering my life in the direction of…

REFLECTION QUESTION

How do you feel about taking responsibility for an area of your life in which you have felt like a victim?
- *unsure if I will be able to truly take back my power*
- *intrigued that I might not be as powerless as I feel*
- *tentatively optimistic*
- *pumped and ready to own it.*

NOTES

Chapter 13
KISS THE GROUND

> *Today, like every other day, we wake up empty*
> *And frightened. Don't open the door to the study*
> *And begin reading. Take down a musical instrument.*
>
> *Let the beauty we love be what we do.*
> *There are a hundred ways to kneel and kiss the ground.*
> **RUMI**

Now we are entering the realms of topography. Let's locate ourselves, as if on a map. We often think of writing as an exercise to know who we are, but we are also always writing to understand *where* we are.

Look down, see where your feet are planted.

> *Walk as if you are kissing the Earth with your feet.*
> **THICH NHAT HANH**

Writing is about locating ourselves in our environment and feeling into the setting of our lives. The setting includes the land we stand on; the history we've inherited; the geographical, historical social spaces that we occupy.

The moment we acknowledge where we are standing, the

question arises: *how did we come to be standing in this place?* For each of us, that is a personal inquiry.

I arrived as an immigrant to Australia in 2001.

Before that, I lived in South Africa. How did I come to be there?

My grandfather left Lithuania in 1924 on a ship to escape anti-Semitism. And so that is where I was born and where I lived the first three decades of my life.

Each one of us has come from somewhere. Many of us have migratory histories. Perhaps your ancestors are indigenous to the land on which you stand. Which is a huge blessing for intergenerational coherence and for access to elders and their wisdom.

Perhaps your ancestors voluntarily migrated from one country to another under circumstances that were not too traumatic. Perhaps they were following a goldrush, or other opportunities.

Perhaps your ancestors were taken as slaves and put on ships and exported across the oceans far away from their homelands through colonialism. These stories of how we come to be on the earth on which we stand, reverberate through us. They either connect us or disconnect us from the land on which we stand.

Did we come to the land as conquerors or slaves?

Did we come in peace? Did we vanquish the indigenous people? Did we steal? Did we take? Did we decide we owned the new land and dispossessed others? Did we come as refugees?

All of these plot lines and storylines converge in the moment that we look down at our feet, notice where we are standing and wonder, *How is it that I come to be occupying the space?*

This inquiry is not intended for any of us to feel shame or guilt – but to simply acknowledge how we come to be where we are. We are not responsible for our ancestors' decisions and actions, but we are responsible for our own, for how we steer our lives going forward.

We are witnesses – because where we stand, and how we occupy space, has a history. We come to notice the ground beneath our feet, the landscape that is the backdrop or our lives.

Is it familiar?

Is it the land of your childhood?

Have you been separated from the land of your childhood?

Do you live in the city surrounded by noise and energies of millions of other human bodies?

Do you live close to the water? At the lip of the ocean? A lake? A river? Under the shadow of a mountain? Near a forest or a desert?

What is the colour of the soil on which you stand?

Do you live in the blazing heat or in icy climates?

Locating ourselves is another act of HINENI, or presence. It expands our proprioception of our environment, the impact we have on our surroundings and the impact that our surroundings have on us.

When I arrived in Australia as an immigrant, I heard the Acknowledgment of Country which I shared at the beginning of this book. It's a beautiful ritual in which you pay your respects to the land on which you stand at any public event. It's a mindful, conscious recognition that the land grants us life. That everything we have – the air we breathe, the food we eat, the water we drink – is a gift from the land. We are indebted to the ecosystem of life that allows us to exist.

You now have the opportunity to communicate with the space in which you find yourself.

Does being where you are bring you a sense of rootedness?

Or are you in a holding pattern, waiting for the right moment in which to leave?

Are you at home?

If not, where is your home?

This inquiry will begin to evoke the question of belonging.

Do you feel as if you belong?

If the answer is no, what would it take for you to feel as if you belong?

Sometimes we belong to a place and we don't realize it.

We only recognize where we belong when we are in exile. It's a funny thing, isn't it?

If you find that you belong to the place where you are in, well, this is a cause for celebration and thanksgiving.

And if you write into a sense of exile, perhaps this chapter will draw you closer to the place that you long to belong to.

Acknowledgement of country and attention to where we are and how we have come to be here is like finding your location on a map. Where is the marker that says home, and how far away from that place are you?

Writing can help us to find our way home. To get back to a place of comfort, safety and belonging. And even if we feel distant from that place – as we describe the distance, how far away we are, the writing brings us close to home again.

So the writing is a way for us to stay close to somewhere that is lost to us.

Today you are writing to help you lose a sense of being lost.

Kahlil Gibran says in *The Prophet*, 'Deep is your longing for the land of your memories.'

Home, I've come to understand, is as much a history as it is a geography. It's a place on the inside that holds us steady, that coiled thread of memories that anchors us to all that has passed.

We humans are funny. We think we can own places.

We talk about owning property and land, but indigenous wisdom teaches us that the land owns us, not the other way around. And so as much as we think we own places, the truth is that places own us. That we belong to a place, rather than a place belongs to us.

It's a little way of turning the idea of ownership of place around. To feel ourselves as being owned by a place.

The poet William Stafford writes, 'Where you live is not crucial, but how you feel about where you live is crucial.'

 **AFFIRMATION**
I am owned by all the places I love.

WRITING SKILL

Setting is a fundamental aspect of the craft of writing. All our stories take place somewhere, even if we don't acknowledge it. Setting is another way that we give meaning to our lives.

We are formed by where we are.

Do we feel safe, anxious, calm, unnerved by being in the city, near the water, rivers, mountains, lakes, oceans, deserts? What we call 'character' or 'personality' is deeply tied to space and place. It's impossible for us to separate ourselves – our longings, dreams, desires, fears and hopes from the places that have formed us.

Places we leave behind become symbolic. We carry places inside us.

Many great fiction writers begin their story with setting – a place – and from that place, they allow characters to emerge, rather than the other way around. Tim Winton says that he always starts with place and lets his stories and characters come from there.

Can you get a sense of how deeply your identity is threaded to a place – either the place you are standing or one you have left behind?

If you write fiction, where you choose to set your story is part of the meaning you are giving to the story. It's not random. Let's take *The Great Gatsby* for example – the setting of that story is significant, the corridor from New York to the suburbs of West Egg (new money) and East Egg (old money). Gatsby's mansion is located in West Egg, which means he is new money. Daisy lives in East Egg, across the water, and the distance that separates him from her is not just the water of the bay but social class. The setting gives meaning to the story too. It show us who is affluent; it demarcates who is poor. The city is where people go to hide their secret lives.

WRITING EXERCISE

Your writing prompt is: The place that I belong to is…

REFLECTION QUESTION

When asked, 'Where are you?' you think of 'where' as:
- *here, in my body*
- *in a room / apartment / house*
- *in my neighbourhood / town / city*
- *in my country.*

NOTES

Chapter 14
TRUST THE UNKNOWN

What happens to perfectly sane people when a flight is delayed?

How unraveled, unruly and stressed does this makes us?

We're like, 'What? This wasn't in my plans… I have somewhere to be… Do you know who I am?'

In day-to-day life, we do everything we can to ensure things go according to our plans. There's no room for accidents, spontaneity or anything that veers off book.

We are addicted to ideas of perfection and being in control.

We want guarantees and warranties.

We want all the holes to be plugged and all the doors to be double-checked.

I mean, after all, we have to-do lists to get through.

All of this is just a way of managing our anxiety.

It is a phony sense of security.

It's a mistake for us to believe our 'arrangements' mean we are in control. At best, our plans are wishes we cast into the Great Mystery – a plea and a whisper, 'Let it come to pass…'

Of course, we can plan, plot, set goals and take right action. This is how we steer our lives and take responsibility for them.

But we also have to be able to trust the unknown.

As an ocean swimmer, I have learned that when a rip pulls you further and further from the shore, the worst efforts you can make is to try to swim against it. Instead, you must surrender, be carried by it, until it returns you in its own time. It is stronger, greater than all our strength and will and muscle.

In writing, we want to be open to the unexpected, that might feel like a rip, pulling us far from safety.

I've always been skeptical about the idea of the 'muse' and the notion of creativity as something outside of us. I prefer to believe writing has more to do with self-discipline (which I can control) than the elusive touch of inspiration, which can't be booked in for an appointment or held to a timeframe.

For many years, I sat myself down in front of my computer every day, irrespective of mood or motivation – and practiced, practiced, practiced, clocking up my ten thousand hours as a writer.

But what I've learned is that there is another aspect to the writing process, an elusive and mercurial energy that is impossible to capture, command and schedule. It is fickle and flighty, late and forgetful. Given that I avoid people like this in my life as a rule, it irks me that I have to indulge these qualities when I write.

But we have to make space for a pop-in by the runaway, the trickster who has no scruples or morals or sense of timing, but who brings a little basket of magic like Little Red Riding Hood, full of goodies. If we don't, we miss – or worse, chase away – the burst of sudden things that can bring our writing to life.

When he delivered his Nobel Lecture in 2005, called 'Art, Truth and Politics,' the playwright Harold Pinter said:

> *I have often been asked how my plays come about. I cannot say. Most of the plays are engendered by a line, a word, or an image that came out of the blue. The first line of* The Homecoming *is 'What have you done with the scissors?' Other than that, I had no further information.*

> *Someone was obviously looking for a pair of scissors and was demanding their whereabouts of someone else he suspected had probably stolen them. But I somehow knew that the person addressed didn't give a damn about the scissors or about the questioner either for that matter.*

I've had a similar experience – while trawling through old letters I'd kept in a box. I came across a thank-you letter from a woman I'd helped many years ago when I worked as a counsellor at a women's crisis centre. Suddenly, an image popped out of the foxhole of my memory, of a woman sitting across the desk from me and I dived for my computer and typed the first sentence of my book *Things Without a Name* – it just opened the floodgates and the whole story came pouring out.

When we write, we need these twin (paradoxical, magnetically opposed) energies. That of steering and self-discipline and that of giving ourselves over to the mystery.

It's a dance, and I admit, I'm easier with the parts I can predict and plot. But I know that if I don't let go of what I 'know,' if I don't surrender to the chaos, I lose the dreaming, the mulling, the trusting-of-the-process part.

We will – and should – be caught off-guard by the direction of muddled things. We cannot helicopter our creativity; we can only offer it the best environment in which it can become itself. And when we get all huffy about the jumble and the anarchy of uncertainty, we can remind ourselves that no-one ever fell in love, or died on time, clocking in.

The turmoil of what we cannot know in advance is also the surreptitious ingredient that lets the mystery in.

Dr Bayo Akomolafe writes, 'Facts oscillate at the speed of mystery.' He teaches that modernity tries to stabilize things – and this is a form of settlement and stems from a colonial mentality. We must be able to be destabilized, to be set off book, to become fugitive. He says we must learn to stay with the troubling emergence of the world and to keep a sense of rupture close.

In everything we do – whether it's writing a book, getting married, having children, immigrating, getting divorced, going through a serious health crisis – we can (and should) prepare ourselves as best we can.

But there's a part that only happens once we're right in the middle of it all – there's a knowing that kicks in when we're riding the storm that we can never access in the lead-up because it only ignites once we're there. And it's *this* deep innerness that we have to learn to trust. The wings we need will grow as we're falling.

Every process and experience has its own mystical quality which we cannot control or predict. At best, we can throw out a question, like a bone into the bushes, and wait for our subconscious mind, like a puppy, to retrieve the answer for us.

Often the answers will come to us, side-on. When we're not overthinking. Maybe in a dream. In a random conversation. A TV commercial.

Over-planning misunderstands the nature of creativity.

The Belgian physical chemist Prigogine won the 1977 Nobel prize in Chemistry, and he was called the 'poet of thermodynamics.'

He was interested in processes such as decay, history, evolution, the creation of new forms and new ideas. He wanted to understand the way things 'become' and believed creation and destruction emerge from the same source.

He talked of irreversible processes in nature which lead both to entropy and to self-organization.

Nature, as we know, is full of hidden patterns and codes – DNA, flowers, insect colonies, fractals, snowflakes. The whole natural world is full of these astonishing secret geometries. Our world is comprised of systems – parts that work together to do a job or are connected to one another.

Some forms in nature are open systems – in constant exchange of energy with the environment – like seeds and plants. Some human systems are also open, like towns, organizations, universities, communities, families. Closed systems do not exchange energy such as rocks, insulated water bottles, refrigerators.

An open system is a dissipative structure. Its structure is maintained by the way in which it allows energy in and out. It is a flowing wholeness, highly organized but always in process.

Now if we take this into thinking about our lives: our lives are open systems. We are constantly bringing new thoughts and energy into them, developing skills, adding, changing, re-arranging. At the same time, our lives are also complex systems – connected at many points and in many ways.

When we write, we are also 'becoming' through that process – we are changing through the writing.

The creative process requires this kind of chaos so that form can emerge.

In an open structure, we can experience instantaneous transitions, jumps in perception, flashes of understanding.

When there is enough disruption, ripples are created throughout the system, creating new connections.

An old pattern can suddenly break, old paradigms can shatter and new ones pop up.

So we have to value disruption, ripples, the state of flux in our lives.

We can learn to trust a burgeoning complexity that at any moment could radically burst into a new order and bring a long-awaited 'structure' to light.

In truth, that structure has been silently in formation in the invisible ventricles of our writing hearts and consciousness.

We have to learn to trust what we cannot yet see, to place our faith in what is, as yet, unknown.

Another way we can trust the unknown is to learn how to wait for something to happen.

In Alaskan Inuit culture, people gather in the darkness and silence, and then they sit and wait for the lyrics of hunting songs to arrive. The men lean into the darkness and silence; and they wait for something to emerge from this womb of uncertainty, this liminal space thresholds, spaciousness, patience and trust.

AFFIRMATION
I trust the unknown.

WRITING SKILL

Much writing happens in bits and pieces – randomly. This is how inspiration works – we connect disparate ideas and suddenly, we have an original idea.

One form I use all the time is the found poem. Poetry is all around us – random phrases, street signs, words spoken by passersby, lines from an SMS, or a Facebook post. As writers, we are collectors of these random pieces. We sew them together and suddenly, they emerge into a strange coherence.

Trusting that there is an organizing intelligence is the key here. Don't overthink it. Have fun.

WRITING EXERCISE

Create a found poem with between 6 – 10 lines.

Capture six random phrases from a book, a previous piece of your writing, the last SMS you received, a random Facebook post, and then put them together as a found poem, trusting that there is some connection amongst these pieces.

Here is an example:

In every corner of your life (birthday card)
Not quite seen (notebook)
Victimized isn't the word (book)
Admitting we are lost (book notes)
Our train goes by (poem)
Paid with love (receipt from my husband)
and plenty of H2O (SMS)

REFLECTION QUESTION

When I think of the unknown, I respond with:
- *Ooh, I love surprises!*
- *Oh no! It's always bad news*
- *I have no control of the unknown*
- *I wish I could predict the future.*

NOTES

Chapter 15
TAKE A STAND

During my lifetime I have dedicated myself to this struggle of the African people. I have fought against white domination, and I have fought against black domination. I have cherished the ideal of a democratic and free society in which all persons live together in harmony and with equal opportunities. It is an ideal which I hope to live for and to achieve. But if needs be, it is an ideal for which I am prepared to die.
NELSON MANDELA,
Pretoria Supreme Court, April 20, 1964

It is never my custom to use words lightly. If 27 years in prison have done anything to us, it was to use the silence of solitude to make us understand how precious words are and how real speech is in its impact on the way people live and die.
NELSON MANDELA,
AIDS conference in Durban, South Africa, July 14, 2000

Writing has helped me to speak up and take a stand on issues that matter to me, like gender violence and climate change.

Words have always been my form of protest, my way of

registering my objections, the tool I have to express my deepest values.

To do this, we need to start by knowing what our values are.

And for some of us, this can be tricky. Because we're overwhelmed with information, overloaded with news, we can feel confused and conflicted about social issues.

The media bombards us with so many different opinions that it may be the hardest work of our lives to know what our deepest values are.

Writing offers us a way to access our beliefs and values so that we can take a stand.

As we write, we begin to sense the shape and form of our deepest values, though they might feel inaccessible to our conscious minds.

Let's acknowledge that we don't start out choosing our beliefs or values. They are instilled in us by our parents and society. We imbibe and absorb them. Many of us live by strong core values without even realizing it – until we make a conscious decision to choose our beliefs and values for ourselves.

When we behave in ways that go against the grain of our deepest core values, we create cognitive dissonance. For instance, if we believe killing animals is wrong, but we eat meat, we are living with a contradiction.

If we believe in gender equality, every time we laugh at a sexist joke or don't speak up against misogyny, we create a crack in our conscience.

Cognitive dissonance causes us to feel:
- anxious,
- embarrassed,
- regretful,

- sad,
- ashamed,
- stressed,
- it impacts on our self-esteem and self-worth.

So we develop behaviours to help us cope and relieve this tension between what we believe and how we act:
- We justify our behaviour – and blame other people or outside factors;
- We pretend and hide our beliefs or behaviours from other people because we're ashamed and feel guilty;
- We only seek out information that confirms our existing beliefs. This is called confirmation bias, and limits our ability to think critically.

So now is a good moment to stop and ask yourself: what are my true core values and beliefs?

Knowing them will fortify your spirit, help you make decisions, keep you steady. You will stop apologizing. You won't be able to be manipulated. In times of uncertainty, people will look to you to see what you're doing.

Remember that fabulous line in the musical *Hamilton* where Hamilton sings, 'If you stand for nothing, Burr, what will you fall for?'

There is a wonderful poem by William Stafford called 'A Ritual to Read to Each Other,' which ends with the lines that encourage those of us who are awake, to be awake, and to ensure that the signals we give – whether they are yes, no or maybe – are unambiguous, because 'the darkness around us is deep.'

In troubling times such as the ones we live in now, we have to be able to take a stand so that we are able to:
- speak up on behalf of others,
- register an objection,
- protest what is unjust and unconscionable,
- say no,
- report a crime,
- start petitions,
- raise awareness,
- set the record straight,
- bear witness to suffering.

These behaviours are a form of spiritual and personal activism – as we keep the vision of life we're committed to alive.

In doing so, we gain personal clarity, we feel a sense of spiritual congruence instead of cognitive dissonance, and we feel a sense of self-respect and dignity.

Our values form our identities. They go beyond our inherited beliefs – the values that mattered in our families of origin: religious values, patriarchal patterns of behaviour, gendered expectations, ideas about sexuality, money.

We can use our words to take a stand or to find what we would fight for.
- What do we believe in?
- What matters to us?
- What would we sacrifice?
- What would we die for?
- Our words help us to draw a line and to pick where we stand.

It's important that we have a sense of what we believe about:
- consumerism, capitalism, wealth accumulation, poverty;
- the role of government in our lives;
- war;
- relationships (including marriage, parenthood, friendships, sexuality, gender, heterosexuality, homosexuality, bisexuality, etc.);
- our responsibility to Nature – including plants, animals, the natural world;
- food (Should we eat meat? Vegetarian? Veganism? Factory farming etc.;
- service, social responsibility versus self-interest and personal achievement;
- nationalism / patriotism;
- religion;
- the education system;
- the value of history and tradition;
- what honesty, truth and justice mean to you;
- the role of the media in society;
- equality (gender, racial, economic etc.).

A combination of our life experience, DNA, nature and nurture is expressed in our views about the world, our attitudes, stances, opinions and beliefs; and these will all be expressed through our writing.

Writing helps us to get clarity about intangible aspects of our lives, and this, in turn, helps us to make decisions.

We can always measure our decisions against the landscape of our values. This clarity helps us to avoid cognitive dissonance and the fractures of the spirit this results in.

This builds our strength. It affirms our agency.

Our values are where we draw a line and set a boundary – this is acceptable, and this is not. This I can live with, and this I will not.

AFFIRMATION

Here is where I draw the line.

WRITING SKILL

Story comes through character – so whenever we write, we are speaking through the voice of a character, even in memoir. Each character has a set of values and boundaries. When we write fiction, we often do a lot of pre-writing to work out who our character is, what they stand for, what they care about and what they are fighting for.

Many of us are spurred to write because we care about an issue – when we start to take shape, almost like a character. We become a person about which others might say, 'She is very principled about recycling,' or 'He doesn't own a car,' or 'She volunteers at a refugee centre.'

Our values make us a certain kind of person – a character with certain traits.

When we write fictional characters, we have to become clear about what the character values and believes so we know how a character would behave or react in certain situation or would not behave in a certain way. Would a character shoplift, give charity, invest in coal mining, buy a sportscar, for example.

Story comes through character, and characters are formed through their beliefs and values which, in turn, impacts on what they say and do.

When you know what your values are, many other decisions in your life become clear because if they conflict with your values, it's much easier to make the decision.

WRITING EXERCISE

Take a moment to close your eyes. To feel your feet on the ground. Your back against a chair or bed. Can you access a sense of your deepest values – what you care about enough that you would be willing to take a stand?

Your writing prompt is: I would be willing to fight for…

REFLECTION QUESTION

When I set a boundary, I feel:
- *clearer about who I am*
- *able to find like-minded people more readily*
- *proud of myself for acting on what I believe*
- *stronger and more readily able to do it again.*

NOTES

Chapter 16
LET IT BE LIGHT

*Nothing is worth more than laughter.
It is strength to laugh and to abandon oneself, to be light.
Tragedy is the most ridiculous thing.*
FRIDA KAHLO

Words can be serious business. But words can also be light.

In this chapter, we are going to explore how we can use our writing for fun, to be silly, playful. For no reason other than to enjoy the way language feels in our mouth and the sensation of it landing in our ears.

Being silly is serious. When we are silly, it:
- reduces stress and anxiety,
- balances hormone levels,
- gives us more energy,
- helps us relax,
- connects us to others,
- helps us find the funny side (there is always a funny side).

When we're little, we seem to know how to play with words.

We roll them over our tongues, feeling their sounds and shapes.

Did you ever repeat a word over and over again, like a mantra, so that it becomes a mesmerizing sound, loosened from meaning?

Bamboozle
Groggy
Oblong
Befuddle
Petticoat
Frangipani
Bugaboo
Tattletale
Smithereens

Words have their own aura that can be split from their meaning. Language can give us goosebumps. Language can thrill us, lift us up on its cadence. Make us feel so alive.

Words can be heavy or light.

What about two words together, which create a joyous sound:

Pitter patter
Jingle jangle
Roly poly
Helter skelter
Chitter chatter

Have you ever taken a word and written it the wrong way round:

> Bedbug – gubdeb
> Rezagrats – stargaze
> Opinion – noinipo

When we do, we create an imaginary language.

Few understood the versatility and richness of language as much as Theodore Geisel, the American children's author, political cartoonist, illustrator, poet, animator, and filmmaker.

We all know him as Dr Seuss.

He was able to tickle our senses with words – he understood cadence and rhyming and the lyricism of language that makes you just want to stand up and read it aloud. It's like a song you want to sing out loud. You want to hear it. You want to be the one to say:

Cos I meant what I said and I said what I meant
An elephant's faithful one hundred per cent.

What I miss most about my children growing up is that they no longer needed me to read Dr. Seuss to them at night. I used to think I did it for them, but when I was no longer needed, I realized how much I loved to read it aloud.

Theodor Geisel changed the way children were being taught to read with the *Dick and Jane* books, which were uninspired and boring.

Geisel was asked to write a book that kids would enjoy reading, but he had to tell the story with just 350 words first-graders would know. Geisel struggled, but finally settled on two words from the list: cat and hat. And in April 1957, *The Cat in the*

Hat was published and became an instant commercial success.

Children's books are wonderful resources for finding language that is joyous, fun, silly and equally profound.

On my bookshelf, I have special shelves reserved for children's books which I was never able to give away even once my children no longer needed them. Whenever I'm feeling as if my language is tired, my thoughts a little bit stale, my use of language boring or unexciting, I just pick up one of these books and read a few pages aloud; and it acts like an effervescent to my thinking and my use of words.

This is your opportunity to connect with the delight of language.

It is easy and fun to generate language that makes us giggle, snicker and laugh out loud.

AFFIRMATION
Silliness is sacred.

Language does more than create meaning. It works with rhyme, onomatopoeia, alliteration and literally ignites our senses.

The way to tell whether something is good for us is to witness the impact it has on our feeling of well-being. Language lights up a certain part of our brain. The lyricism, alliteration, rhyming, gives us the same flushes of chemicals we get when we listen to music.

Here are some ideas for you.

Find a word that has a great noun sound in it – and brainstorm all the words that rhyme with it:

The ooze of the news
brings 7 o'clock blues
I'd rather snooze
Or have some booze
We do not choose
Our own true views
When we turn on the news.

Take a letter of the alphabet and use it to write a whole paragraph – every word or second word should start with the letter.

I wrote a poem for a collection of poems called *The Alphabet of Women* and I was given the letter J. Here are the first few stanzas:

Just a perfect girl
with jet black hair
my parents' jackpot
Joanne they chose
for 'Gracious is Jehovah'
named to be
a four-leafed clover.

Jutted up to be
jolly tall
'juvenile jailbait'
I heard them call.

Jibed about
my Jewish nose
but kept it giant,
never to be
beauty-reliant.

Pick a letter of the alphabet and see how far you take it – using as many words as you can starting with that letter.

Here's a fun poem I wrote using rhyme and alliteration

Wisdom

The guru was grimy
The shaman was shmarmy
The vicar smelt of liquor
The rabbi was a rogue
The maven was craven
The doctor was degenerate
The poet was a poser
The expert, an extortioner
The mentor was manic
The specialist was lecherous
The professor, a poor dresser,
The healer was a hedonist
The minister was sinister,
The monk was a punk
And the princess, couldn't care less
But the sunrise didn't lie
Or try to sell me anything.

WRITING SKILL

Here are parts of speech which opens up fun and playful ways of using language:

> *Onomatopoeia* – words that sound like the thing they are:
> - tweet, slurp, bang, crash, whisper, jingle, squash
> - machine noises: honk, beep, vroom, clang, zap, boing
> - boom, crash, whack, thump, bang
> - shush, giggle, growl, whine, murmur, blurt, whisper, hiss
>
> *Assonance* – repetition of a vowel sound:
> - 'to let the cat out of the bag,' 'how now brown cow,' 'high in the sky,' 'below the streetlamps I go,' 'slow, black, crow-black, fishing boat, bobbing sea,' 'tiger tiger burning bright, in the forest of the night'
>
> *Alliteration* – repetition of a consonant:
> - 'fair is foul and foul is fair,' 'the tree swayed steadily in the summer sun'

WRITING EXERCISE

Frida Kahlo wrote, 'I heaven you.' She took a noun and she turned it into a verb.

> Make a list of nouns you love – for example:
> - *French fries*
> - *Sunrise*
> - *Rainbow*
> - *Flamingo*
> - *Kitten*
> - *Weeping willow*
> - *Waffle*

Turn those nouns into verbs:
- *I want to French fries you with kisses*
- *You weeping willow me*
- *I am flamingo-ed by your touch*
- *She was kittened in kindness*
- *She was waffled by his attention.*

REFLECTION QUESTION

Play feels:
- *frivolous*
- *essential to my wellbeing*
- *a waste of time when I could be doing something useful*
- *creatively inspiring.*

NOTES

Chapter 17
GO WILD

People run from rain but sit in bathtubs full of water
CHARLES BUKOWSKI

Creativity doesn't thrive in captivity.

Our creative life force bursts from a primal vitality that is deeply connected to the wildness inside us. The part of us that is a little unkempt: unruly, maybe even indecent and obscene.

Most of us have learned that to be respectable, decent, civilized members of society, we have to sacrifice and relinquish aspects of our deliciously wild selves.

So we domesticate our animal instincts.

We learn manners. Social norms.

We tame ourselves with housework, matching linen, interior décor, laundry, to-do lists, agendas and schedules. When these are the cornerstones of our lives, they rob us of our rapture and our creativity.

We fold ourselves inwards, tuck away our rawness, smooth our edges.

We become ever so nice, polite, genteel.

We work hard to be accepted, to fit in, maintain a reputation, keep up appearances. In the process, we become dented with decency, cramped and crimped with civility and conventionality.

We lose our lustre, our lust for life. We become pastel instead of luminous.

The author Tom Robbins encourages writers not to have too much furniture, but rather to sit on wooden boxes or the floor. He claims that being too comfortable makes us dull and unoriginal.

My life changed in my early twenties when I read Clarissa Pinkola Estes' book *Women Who Run with the Wolves*. She reminds us that deep in our veins, we are part of a rich and magical world in which we are free and uncensored. But we must be willing to be wild.

In this chapter, we are going to explore the ways in which we are tame and how we can learn from the wilderness. We ask it to share its secrets with us.

We must reconnect with the earth so that we can remain grounded, the fluidity of water so we can flow and keep moving forward, the power of fire so we can transform, and the lightness of wind and sky so that we can hold everything the world brings to us.

The wildness is our teacher.

What has taken the wild from us? Colonialism, capitalism, consumerism, patriarchy, religion – they have all contributed to the fantasy that humans exist outside the natural world and that the natural world is ours to do what we want with.

We have been taught this very strange business of *owning* things.

Everything we touch, we say, 'Mine,' without thinking that

we are part of everything we touch.

As a result, we have exploited the land; polluted the environment; and visited unimaginable cruelties in the names of science, commerce and human desire.

Today we have the chance to explore the ways in which domestication and civility have tamed the wildness out of us.

In this watering down of ourselves, this dilution of our wild nature, we have become dumb and forgetful. We have lost our ability to attune to sounds that are not language.

The natural world is alive. It speaks to us, but we have stopped being able to hear what it is saying.

Ralph Waldo Emerson wrote:

> *Earth may be alive... alive like a tree. A tree which quietly exists, never moving, except to sway in the wind yet endlessly conversing with the sunlight and the soil.*

Bill Neidjie AO (c. 1913–2002), a Gagadju man, was the traditional custodian of the Kakadu area of the Northern Territory of Australia and an indigenous elder.

He wrote: 'Tree, he watching you. You look at tree, he listen to you. He got no finger, he can't speak, but that leaf, he pumping, he growing, growing in the night, While you sleeping, you dream something. Tree and grass, same thing.'

We no longer know how to follow the tracks of creatures underwater or on land, how to find water, to understand the ways birds call and answer to one another, the sighs of the grass, the exhalations of the mountains, the whispers of clouds.

This wildness is all around us, but we have forgotten how to connect with it.

Sometimes we remember and we:
- skinny-dip,
- dive through a wave in the ocean,
- walk through a track in a forest,
- hike up a mountain,
- make fire,
- drum,
- chant,
- dance,
- walk in the rain.

e. e. cummings wrote that the world is 'mud-luscious' and 'puddle-wonderful.'

We need to move away from the roof over our heads, get wet, get dirty, feel our hungers and our thirsts.

Stray from the mediocre middle.

Shimmy towards an edge, some place where we feel something primal and raw.

Those of us who have been through childbirth might know this wildness.

Sex can take us there.

Cooking food over fire, baking bread, eating with our fingers, sleeping under the stars.

The wild fuels our creativity and passion. It is the antithesis of the over-tamed, muffled, respectable, pruned conventionality we are all trapped in.

When we howl, crave, lust, scream, cry, become profane, blasphemous, we touch the wildness once more.

AFFIRMATION
I will not be tamed.

We can nurture every opportunity to return to the wildness inside ourselves.

We do this by remembering the inter-corporeality between humans and the rest of nature. We too are part of nature, so even talking about the 'natural world' as something outside of us separates us ideologically from our source.

But the nitrogen, calcium, iron and carbon that are in our bones and blood and teeth are all derived from the cosmos, from the stars. We are made of the same stuff as everything else under the sun.

Yet somehow, we have managed to forget this and to raise ourselves above all the other creatures and imagine that human life is more intelligent, more important and more valuable than that of plants and animals and the living, breathing, heaving world of dust and rain and cloud.

I invite you now to reconnect with your wild nature through your writing.

Nature is burgeoning with deep intelligence and beauty from which we have cut ourselves off.

We have so much to learn from the wild. To be a student, we must be humble.

Every day, when I swim from the shore into the wide-open waters of the ocean, I am conscious of being just another creature in the sea. I am not special because I am human. I am just another body in the water. I feel so small and at the same time, so enlarged and connected to all life in those moments when my humanity is just a speck, when I'm at the mercy of waves and rips and tides, and other much larger creatures out there.

WRITING SKILL

When we write, we always write from a particular point of view. Point of view is the 'eye' or narrative voice of a piece of writing.

Whenever we write, we must not forget that we are claiming a specific vantage point.

We are always writing from a subjective point of view.

Subjectivity always comes with a set of beliefs and assumptions. There is no such thing as an 'ideological virgin.' This is a phrase used by Judge Edwin Cameron to describe how judges on the bench always come with assumptions, world views and prejudices.

When we look at the world, we must remember that our eyes have been tamed.

We can shift points of view and see the world through wild eyes.

I once saw a sign on a beach that read:

On the beach and in the sea, animals do not leave trash – humans do. Please behave like animals.

Gary Larson cartoons often invert the perspective we expect. One of his cartoons shows a pair of crabs on a beach looking at two babies, and the one says to the other one, 'Yes, they're quite strange during the larval stage.'

Tom Robbins, in his book *Skinny Legs and All*, includes a cast of characters including a Conch Shell, Painted Stick, a Sock, a Spoon, and a Can O'Beans.

WRITING EXERCISE

Your writing prompt is: What am I? (not 'Who am I?')

The word 'what' is a cue to remind us that we too are made of carbon and nitrogen and iron. Our atoms and particles are no different from the tree, the fish in the ocean or the kangaroo.

REFLECTION QUESTION

What impact has the taming of your wild self had on your life?
- *I have made safe choices*
- *I have stayed in one place for too long*
- *I have never explored my creativity or sexuality*
- *I never rely on my instincts or intuition.*

NOTES

Chapter 18
CONFESS

What is the one story in your life you're most afraid someone will find out? What incident in your past still haunts you?

We all have those secreted parts of ourselves, bottled up, buried, stuffed into our internal closets, hidden away from view.

We're all hiding something.
- a shame;
- a regret;
- guilt – for an infidelity, a termination, illicit liaison, act of violence, sexual encounter, hurtful thing we said or loving word we didn't offer, trick we played that went wrong;
- an addiction we can't shake.

We're all holding grief and sorrow for our mistakes.

Sometimes we have forbidden thoughts:
- Maybe you feel you married the wrong person; you missed the boat; you're in the wrong relationship.
- Maybe you have sexual desires, hopes and dreams that don't conform with your sense of who you are.

- Do you regret having had children or not having had children?
- Maybe you are hiding an addiction, or nursing a grief in the closet of your history.
- Perhaps you feel unworthy or not good enough because of something you did or something that was done to you.
- Maybe there are times when you feel an imposter despite all your credentials, skills and experience.

Not a single one of us escapes childhood perfectly intact.

We are all hurt and hurting because that is what it means to be human. And there is no shame in any of it.

But these feelings become stowaways in our psyche, and they form part of our shadow. They reside in the darkness, become the dark twin, the disowned or repressed self, the id. They become demons, the devil inside. They take us through the dark night of the soul and into the underworld.

The American poet laureate Robert Bly called the shadow 'the long bag we drag behind us.'

As we grow, whatever doesn't fit our idealized sense of self or who we want to be becomes our shadow.

But Jung reminded us that we can never elude the shadow. It is a 'primordial part of our human inheritance.' Whenever these emotions surge through us, these gross, ghastly gremlins, we feel guilty and ashamed. We renew our efforts to suffocate them with more murderous intent.

So how does the shadow manifest if it's so well hidden?

Whenever we dislike a trait in someone else or are repelled by certain kinds of people, our shadow beckons. If our idealized self is obedient and responsible, we may find that we sometimes act out of character (a cue to investigate).

Other clues are feelings of contempt, disgust or reprehension towards others. Projection.

As soon as we dehumanize or demonize other races, genders, religions or people who are unlike us, we're working in our own shade.

This is how our shadow leaves a trail of breadcrumbs. And if we are brave enough and willing to enter the forest, we may learn something about ourselves that will help solve the puzzle of our identities. Of course, this can be scary.

Robert Bly writes, 'We spend our life until we're twenty deciding what parts of ourselves to put into the bag, and we spend the rest of our lives trying to get them out again.'

We can write as a way of leading ourselves into this forest.

As we write, we can touch and be touched by our shadows.

All of us have edges, taboos, places inside that scare us.

We cannot tell the truth or write from a place of self-knowledge without embracing this murky terrain and bringing responsible awareness to aspects of ourselves that we have kept in the dark.

Jung wrote:

One does not become enlightened by imagining figures of light, but by making the darkness conscious.

He paid special attention to the work of integrating the shadow and claimed it was an initiation to an awakened life, an essential awareness for our self-realization. We can bring a lantern into these unlit territories through our writing.

We can write to heal the split between our conscious sense of self and who we might be. When we integrate the shadow, we create a unifying awareness. We balance the paradox, allow for ambiguity.

Here is a poem I once wrote called 'Do Not Do No Harm':

Do not be
harmless
as the Buddhists teach.
There is no grit in goodness.
No pearl without sand.
No butterfly whose wings
have not been distressed.

You must break promises
to yourself and others;
do the unforgiveable;
torture those you love;
hunt the fox
and then eat
its fear-stained flesh.
All this you must do
to learn that there is nowhere to go
no one to become unless you
turn your face
towards the threat inside you.
Not until you learn
where you are jagged
brutal
irredeemable
will you become
visible to yourself.

This is what it means
to be alive:
to know your harm
like you know the freckles
on your skin;
mottles of imperfection
as guilty of sin as
the San Andreas Fault.

Like the earth is torn
you are torn.
Like it is broken
so are you.

To do no harm
is to
shrink from shadow
as if it weren't
in you,
from you,
like the outbreath.

It's our shadows that make us fascinatingly, deeply, beautifully human.

 **AFFIRMATION**
I am not ashamed by any part of who I am.

When we write into this part of ourselves, the most important mandate is that we do not judge ourselves. This writing engages radical self-compassion. We're simply exploring an aspect of who we are out of curiosity in the service of understanding ourselves more fully. With the aim of loving ourselves more completely.

In this chapter, we are chasing shadows.

What are you afraid to know or understand about yourself?

In 2004, Frank Warren invited people to post him their secrets on homemade postcards when he began a community art project in the United States. He was overwhelmed by the response as hundreds of thousands of people all over the world sent in their secrets. Thus began PostSecret, which has become an international phenomenon, including a series of books and a blog. Here are some of the secrets:

> *Sometimes I think that if I just got really sick, I'd find out who my true friends are.*
>
> *My dog winks at me sometimes. I always wink back in case it's some sort of code.*
>
> *When we're on a business trip together, I secretly hope a random stranger will remark what a great couple we are and that will make you see we should be a couple.*

Secrets reveal dimensions of human frailty. As we identify with the shame, regret, anxiety, sadness or joy in them, we start to feel a space open inside us where we feel safe to be vulnerable.

PostSecret created an anonymous community of acceptance, which has in turn helped many people accept themselves.

A secret can become a prison for the soul, a way of staying hidden from others and ourselves, in what author and medical intuitive Caroline Myss has termed 'woundology,' where we allow our wounds to control us.

Confession in various religious forms acknowledges that the truth does indeed set us free. As Frank Warren of PostSecret says, 'Sometimes when we think we are keeping a secret, that secret is actually keeping us.'

When we share our secrets, we begin to heal from shame.

But we cannot heal what we do not acknowledge.

Trust in relationships accrues when our secrets are held with tenderness by others. When we are loved in all our naked imperfection, we learn that we are worth loving, and we make it safe for others to share their secrets with us. The poet Adrienne Rich says when we tell the truth, we create the possibility for more truth around us.

WRITING SKILL

The writing skill that relates to this theme is subtext.

Subtext is the silent language underneath the spoken language – what people are really saying. It's the difference between what we say and what we really mean.

People who are sexually attracted to each other are talking about coffee. 'I really like it strong and hot.' What is actually being said?

Or, 'You never remember to take out the garbage,' when someone is saying, 'I think I don't love you anymore.'

When someone asks, 'How are you?' and you say, 'I couldn't be better,' when what you really want to say is, 'I am lonely.'

How subtext peeks through is when people's words and their actions or expressions don't match. That's how subtext ruptures or breaches the surface of meaning.

WRITING EXERCISE

The secret I want to confess is…

REFLECTION QUESTION

Telling my secret made me feel:
- *vulnerable and ashamed*
- *liberated*
- *like I am no longer pretending or lying*
- *much more of an interesting human being.*

NOTES

Chapter 19
PLAY WITH FIRE

When I was in my forties, I decided to go for swimming chapters to get some stroke correction. My teacher taught me how to position my elbow, keep my fingers slightly apart and to breathe, not on every third stroke, but whenever I needed to.

At one point, he said to me, 'I can only take a student so far.'

'What do you mean?' I asked.

And he said, 'It's one thing to teach someone the correct posture and movement, but I cannot teach the most important part of swimming, which is how your body feels in the water. That's something each person has to find out on their own. It's a very personal relationship, how our arms, legs and torso feel moving through water. No-one can tell you how to feel at home in the water.'

The author, Jorge Luis Borges, wrote, 'Art is fire plus algebra.'

What does he mean?

The algebra is the craft of writing – which is something each of us can learn. We can be taught story structure, character arc, how to edit and so on. The writing tips that I'm sharing with you in this book is the 'algebra' of writing, if you like.

But the fire… that is something we each have to find for ourselves. It cannot be taught.

Our own fire is the place inside us that burns brightly, that is deeply ignited by the things we care about.

It's the home of our emotions, the coven of our passions.

So when we play with fire, we're looking for where and in what ways we are passionate.

I'm not talking just about romance, lust, love and sex. We're exploring the full range of our passions. What stirs our hearts. What makes us feel alive, enlarged, enraged, powerful, powerless.

Albert Camus wrote, 'Live to the point of tears.' Passion is about living at that edge of emotion.

Many of us work hard to repress our emotional lives.

Perhaps we were told as children that we were over-sensitive, and that we needed to become more thick-skinned. That was the refrain of my childhood because I used to cry about everything. Every tragedy and injustice that I heard about, I took very personally. I couldn't seem to separate myself from.

Perhaps our feelings were not witnessed, seen, heard or met. So we learned that they were unimportant, trivial, and we hid them away.

Many of us – women in particular – repress our anger. In my book *Unbecoming*, I have a chapter called The Burning Woman – which is about how when I turned fifty, I got in touch with an emotion I had repressed my whole life – rage:

I had never known rage. Passion, yes, but not anger. 'A temper is not very attractive on a lady,' my granny Bee would say when I'd express a strident opinion or raise my voice. So I'd adjusted myself.

But with menopause, everything changed.

Vagueness, a *not-sure-what-do-you-think?* people-pleasing personality trait lest I not be liked by the average so-and-so, vanished. Everything blurry clicked into sharp focus, like a lens in those optometry frames which turns an O into a D.

My anger, like an arterial stent, purified and cleansed me, not in a holy-mother-of-god-virginal way, but in a near-death-gasping-for-breath-skin-melting apocalypse that stripped me raw. It aroused a dormant voice, an echo stirred from where voice began; it brought the silent war inside out. I was The Burning Woman, not one tied to the stake and set alight by those who feared her, but one with a fire rising from her belly, marking where the kingdom of herself began and where it ended. It became my firewall, a fortification. Admittedly, it was not me at my most amiable or amenable. But it was me at my most powerful, and it both thrilled and terrified me.

If we feel contracted, quietened, small, accessing our anger is a way for us to break free.

We become bigger when we access this fire energy, this energy of the Hindu goddess Kali.

Kali is the goddess of change and destruction. You'd recognize her as a blue, multi-armed figure with a garland of skulls.

In this chapter, I invite you to play with fire.

Fire is part of our primal nature – generates heat, it wards off the darkness.

It consumes other elements – wood, coal, paper.

It is the transformer – it converts other objects into heat, light, ash and smoke. It is used for rituals of protection, courage, sex, to energize, for strength and to banish negativity. It purifies. But as much as we are drawn to its warm, bright, beckoning beauty, we must come with respectful caution. It has to be controlled because it can be dangerous and unpredictable.

This is one of the qualities of living a passionate life. It's quite edgy. If we are living a neat, tidy and dutiful existence, we may start to feel the need to live closer to the edge; and we might end up doing something destructive – taking risks that imperil us or others.

Living a passionate life raises important questions about our relationship with danger and taboo – all of which are important questions in every human life – questions about the risks we are willing to take.

A passionate life is one in which we embrace change.

Kali energy destroys.

It destroys beliefs that no longer serve us.

Kali destroys everything that is not love.

It gives us a fiery courage to do things that take us out of a place that has become overgrown and is too safe and comfortable.

Growth is essential in life – and especially in a spiritual life.

We can never be complacent and imagine that we have reached the zenith of our growth and okay, let's make camp here and never leave.

The fire of Kali:
- dissolves our limiting beliefs,
- fortifies our strength and courage,
- breaks down fear and ego,
- stokes our sexuality and sensuality.

Eros, passion and rage are all aspects of our fire energy.

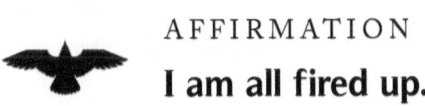
AFFIRMATION
I am all fired up.

WRITING SKILL

When your writing feels stale, dull, flat, ordinary, we have a saying, 'Move towards the fire,' or 'Follow the fire.'

It's about finding a vein, where we feel some heat, and this has to do with the furnace of our emotions.

Natalie Goldberg, the writing teacher, says, 'Just enter the heat of words and sounds and colored sensations and keep your pen moving across the page.'

Our aim is always to write from the place where our fire burns, or perhaps if we cannot feel that place yet, we can write towards it.

Maybe you don't want to write about your heartache, but can you try to write from it. We each have our own fire energy which can fuel our writing. And the quality of it is palpably different from writing that is over-thought, that comes from our heads rather than our bellies.

As if you were on fire from within.
The moon lives in the lining of your skin.
PABLO NERUDA

This fire energy is about accessing what you care deeply about. What gets you furious, aroused, provoked – enough to feel something burning inside you.

If you don't feel this way about anything, perhaps this is your chance to be curious and wonder why you feel neutral about everything when there are so many injustices and so much suffering in the world. What part of you is defended, submerged, shut down?

WRITING EXERCISE

I am enraged by… I am aroused by…

REFLECTION QUESTION

> **The fire inside me:**
> - *makes me feel sexually alive and sensually vibrant*
> - *is a rage against injustice*
> - *fuels my creative work*
> - *is a destructive force in my relationships.*

NOTES

Chapter 20
GO BACK FOR THE ORPHANS

There's a beautiful poem by *Geffrey Davis* called 'What I Mean When I Say Farmhouse.' In that poem he takes us back to a moment in his childhood through the senses of smell and sounds, and he finds himself as a boy, and he writes that he wants to go back through the years to find the child he was, and to 'write less fear into the boy running through the half-dark.' This line just cuts straight into my heart, 'I've come for the boy.'

I love this poem so much for the image of the adult who has survived and knows exactly where his suffering began, where the pain of his past sits. I am moved to tears at the image of him trawling backwards to find that small, scared child; and by finding him with language, he extricates the pain and terror that little person experienced.

We have all got places inside ourselves where something happened that hurt us – and these places have an energy and life force. If we tap into them, they can become a source of our own creativity.

It may be:
- a moment that brought you to your knees;
- a time when you didn't know if you would be able to go on;
- a time when you first remember feeling a powerful emotion like fear, anxiety, loneliness, anger, hatred, regret.

So how do we write into difficult places?

What you've probably realized by now is that you have come to writing precisely because your soul knows you need to revisit those places.

If you have always wanted to write, there is a story, maybe more than one story, inside of you that has called you back to that place. And it is likely a difficult story. It's a story that has persisted and continued to poke you in your dreams, wrestle your subconscious mind, and remind you, 'Don't forget.' Don't forget this place. Come back, come back, come back here. But because it is a painful place, we are masters at finding distractions and trajectories that lead us anywhere but back to that place.

But there comes a time when those routes haven't taken us anywhere closer to peace or wholeness. We have been circling around that difficult place for so long. We know that there really is only one option left to us – and that is to go inwards, to go into that place. Writing can help us enter there.

When you go into that place, you will need a lantern, a shovel and a big brave heart. You need a lantern to light your way. You need a shovel because it's likely that you're going to have to dig up some ground. You're going to have to excavate. Whatever it is you're writing about is not sitting there neatly on top, perched on a little mound for you to reach in and take it. This job we have to do is archaeological. Sometimes we're not even quite sure what we're digging for. We just know it's somewhere in there.

And we need a big brave heart because we know that it's not going to be an easy road.

It's important to come to this writing at a time when we feel resourced. Don't go into the writing when you are exhausted emotionally, or you're feeling particularly fragile and vulnerable or unsupported. Only undertake this journey when you feel sturdy. Having a meditation or some kind of spiritual practice will give us that sense of sturdiness.

I'm going to talk you through how I have written into some of the very painful places in my own story in the hope that it will guide and help you to do the same.

This is how I do it.

First of all, I know the moment I'm aiming for. I know the direction I'm heading in.

I then make sure there are no distractions around me. It takes so much emotional energy to walk into those dark woods. The last thing you want is for the phone or doorbell to ring, to pull you out just as you are approaching something difficult to get close to.

Then I light a candle. It's the visual manifestation of a lantern, because writing into a wounded place is a sacred act of the soul.

Then I might throw out a little prayer, asking for help to get there. I ask the universe, my ancestors, my guides, the muse – however one wants the divine to show up – just to be with me, to guide me, hold me close to this place, help me to find my way in.

So I make sure I have set everything up first.

And the reason is, writing into difficult places is not a casual business. And so I come to it with a certain measure of sanctification, seriousness, resolution of the spirit, humility, asking for help, guidance, clarity, strength and wisdom.

And once that is all done, I close my eyes and I lean back. I allow myself to fall backwards into that moment. I'm aiming for that feeling of vertigo, to pull me back into that moment I have tried to dodge or pretend, 'Oh, it wasn't so bad. Really. You know, it happens to all of us. We all go through difficult things.'

You know, the things we say to help us get through. And I always clear away all of that noise, the noise that I've created around the moment and really let myself feel it all over again.

I see myself back in that moment. I try to see some details, the sensory details – the weather, was I hot? Cold? What was I wearing? Who was there? What colors, smells, sounds, tastes made up that moment. I try to re-enter my body as it was then. My body is holding that memory for me. I start with just one sensory detail I can hold on to. And I simply write into that sensory detail.

'It was dawn and the phone rang. A shrill, piercing sound. I opened my eyes and I looked at my watch. It was twenty to six in the morning. Who was phoning at this time?'

The sound of that phone.

And I will go back into that moment and write into the way my heart started to hammer in my chest. That strange shrill, piercing sound that happens inside your ear as adrenaline starts to coarse through your veins and you know that you're about to hear something you don't want to hear. And I will write back into as much of that moment in my body as I can and capture it.

Now, what you will find is that as you write into your senses, the emotion of that moment will start to pierce through. It will ooze into your writing. As you allow the soft fluid of that moment to fill up all the space, write into that emotion as close as you can. You might be able to name the emotion – fear, dread, terror. But you don't have to, because if you simply stay with how the emotion worked in your body, you will be showing us the emotion.

But you can also name the emotion and give it sounds, smells, tastes, textures, colors. Then enter that memory fully as if you are now right back in it and tell – then what happened? And then? And then? And then?

Take some deep breaths.

By this time, if you have tapped a vein, touched a nerve, you will be filled with all kinds of emotions. You'll be feeling the energy and emotion all over again.

Fear.

Terror.

Grief.

Loss.

You'll know if you've touched the nerve if you find yourself crying. Don't be afraid of the emotion that comes up. Just meet it. With kindness and compassion.

If you feel overwhelmed with emotion, you are reliving that emotion. That's why it is so important for you to feel resourced because you are now coming back to that, that emotion.

But this time you're doing it consciously.

The first time, it was thrust upon you. You were not ready for it. You didn't know what to expect. And that is why it was such a trauma and a shock.

But now you are going back in as a guide. You know where you're going. You've got your lantern. You've got your shovel and your big brave heart. The thing is that you survived. And now you're coming back to it as a survivor. You're going to survive it again.

So you go into that moment. Let it be. Let it arrive on the page. Take some deep breaths; let yourself cry. The moment will flare, and then, the emotion will subside like a sigh.

This is not the end of it.

But it is how you begin.

There is one more step.

In a later chapter, I will teach you the choreography of it. But for now, this is as far as we go.

AFFIRMATION
I will leave no-one behind.

Here is a poem I wrote for some of the writers I have mentored:

In That Place

When you find it
Come back and tell us.
What did you see in that starless dark?
What heavens deserted you
and how did you survive
those broken nights
in the jungle
not knowing if you would ever
be found again?
How did you crawl from your bed
In the days beyond grief?
Who did you become
after they left you for dead
six of them, you said?
With what did you mend
and stitch yourself whole
and return to love without
ever having received it?
Take your precious beauty back

along those abandoned tracks
when you get there
let your voice rise
shout your name
In that place you are
strong, my friend.
Go this time to name
by what curious grace
you came back once.
You will never get lost there again.

WRITING EXERCISE

What part of yourself do you need to go back to retrieve?
Writing prompt: I'm going back for...

REFLECTION QUESTION

The thought of going back to painful places in my past:
- *feels terrifying – why would I voluntarily feel that pain again?*
- *is a rescue mission – I know I have to retrieve myself*
- *feels empowering – I want to feel whole*
- *is never going to happen. I survived and that's all that matters.*

NOTES

Chapter 21
ASK FOR HELP

We all strive to be independent. We're told this is what it means to be a well-adjusted adult.

We work hard to stay in control.
We learn how to fix things.
We read the instruction manuals.
We do lots of self-help.
We read the books.
Do the meditations.
We don't need assistance, support, any kind of aid.
We've got this.

From when I was a little girl, I was expected to fend for myself and grow up quickly.

So I learned – to self-soothe and rely on no-one but me.

And I was always very proud of the fact that I was so self-sufficient, that I didn't need anyone. I could do it alone.

It was only as an adult, after some therapy, that I understood that to be so unhelp-able, so radically independent and flagrantly capable is actually a trauma response.

It's the result of never having had anyone come to my rescue.

It's a survival strategy – we do everything for ourselves because when we were needy, no-one was there.

Just sit with this for a moment and see if this resonates for you in anyway.

I am terrible at asking for help.

I have to be completely incapacitated before I can admit that I might need a hand. Asking for help makes me feel needy, vulnerable, pathetic, incompetent.

Asking for help can feel like failure because we have to:
- be humble enough to say – actually, I don't know what to do, or I can't do this on my own;
- give up control;
- override our egos;
- surrender to an unknown outcome;
- bow to the great mystery;
- acknowledge, 'I'm undone here, I can't fix this, I'm all out of answers… please help.'

Just to let you know – I am getting better at this – but I've had to have some serious downfalls to learn how to ask for help. And it's only a few select people in my life who would ever know that I was struggling or needed support of any kind.

I've come to think of asking for help as a form of prayer.

Sometimes the prayer is:

Help me to have wisdom in this moment, to say or do the right thing

Help me to be brave

Help me to have less fear

Help my heart to stay open

Help me to survive this heartache

Help me to have intuition

Help me to be kind

Help me to want my life

Help me to forgive

Help me to let go.

Some of us might reach a point in our lives where we're asking for help to go on, to keep enduring, to keep taking another breath.

When we ask for help, we're usually addressing our God, or gods, the angels, or we're tapping into the Akashic records.

But even if we don't come from a culture which has a strong tradition of invoking ancestral spirits, we can still call for guidance from those who have come before us.

We've all inherited genetic traits from our parents who inherited theirs from their parents, who inherited theirs from their parents, and so on, and so on, and so on to the beginning of time.

The blood of our ancestors runs in our veins.

More recently, we're acknowledging that it's not only genes and artefacts that are handed down to us from our ancestors, but their emotions and traumas.

Epigenetics is a fascinating field of study that opens up a conversation between our emotional and psychological worlds and those of our forebears.

The past lives inside us as genetic material, but also as experiences, anxieties, fears and stories.

The field of family constellations and epigenetic inheritance is enthralling. I encourage you to investigate it further if the resonance of this feels powerful for you. It certainly has been for me.

Sometimes we may not understand the source of a particularly stubborn anxiety or addictive behaviour. Maybe we spend years working to eradicate it, yet it persists no matter what healing we attempt. It may be an irrational anxiety that seems to have no source in any life experience we can pinpoint or remember, or an addiction that we cannot budge.

These may be inherited from an ancestor.

The key research that has been done around this phenomenon involved mice which were exposed to the smell of cherry blossom at the same time as an electric shock was administered.

What was discovered was that five generations of mice later, mice that were exposed to the smell of cherry blossom released the same cortisol from fear and anxiety that the mice who had had shocks administered. So the smell of cherry blossom, which became associated with a shock, was handed down as genetic memory to five generations of mice later.

Many of us have ancestors who experienced some form of slavery, genocide or trauma, and so perhaps the memories of those experiences still live somewhere inside of us.

I was overwhelmed with emotion when I first came across this research about a decade ago. See, for most of my life, I could never understand why I had such debilitating and overwhelming fear of dying young. I was terrified I would leave my children motherless when they were very young.

It was only when I started doing research into my ancestry and I found that not only did my father's mother die when he was just 13, but my great grandmother on my mother's side died at 36 of tuberculosis.

So on both sides of my family tree were mothers who were sickly and who abandoned their children when they were very young.

As soon as I had that information, something in me released and relaxed, and I felt for the first time as if the fear

I was carrying, the source of which I could never understand, was perhaps not mine. Perhaps I was carrying it on behalf of an ancestor.

Stephi Wagner, author of *Motherhood Reclaimed: Healing the Motherwound*, writes, 'Pain travels through families until somebody is willing to feel it.'

AFFIRMATION

I am willing to feel the pain for all those who have suffered before me.

Being willing to feel the pain that our ancestors have experienced, and to acknowledge what has been lost, is a real act of showing up not only on behalf of yourself but on behalf of the soul of your entire extended family.

Our ancestors live inside of us.

Do you remember that moment in the *Lion King* where Rafiki tells Simba, 'He lives in you, your father. He lives in you'?

In this chapter, we are writing to ask for help from an ancestor – perhaps it is one we knew and lost, or even one we have even never met. This is a way of reconnecting some of the spiritual and emotional dots in our psyches and our families' histories.

Our ancestry is not only a genetic inheritance but a narrative inheritance, and an emotional bequest, a psychic baton that is handed to us consciously or unconsciously.

What did those who came before us know? What do they want us to know? Who are we because of them and their sacrifices? These are the questions that belong to today's inquiry.

Experiences in the past cause an electric current of emotional energy to pass through us. It's what we call emotional valence and causes a reaction in our bodies – our throat may tighten, we may feel dizzy or we may get a pain in our chest.

WRITING SKILL

Let's experiment with using the first, second and third person so you can feel how the valence of a sentence can change and our proximity to the heat of the emotion.

First person: *I fear dying young. I am so afraid that my life will be cut short and I will not get to live out the full length of my days. I will leave my children before they are old enough to know how to navigate the world.*

Second person: *You fear dying young. You are so afraid that your life will be cut short and you will not get to live out the full length of your days. You will leave your children before they are old enough to navigate the world.* ('You' incorporates the person reading it.)

Third person: *She feared dying young. She was so afraid that her life would be cut short and she would not get to live out the full length of her days. She would leave her children before they were old enough to navigate the world.*

We create a prism in which we can separate ourselves from our fear, get some distance by using the second person and even more distance by using the third person.

WRITING EXERCISE

Address an ancestor and ask that ancestor for help with something you have not been able to resolve in your own life. Speak to them directly: 'I don't know what to do about…'

REFLECTION QUESTION

Asking for help makes me feel:
- *helpless, like a victim – as if I can't do things for myself*
- *human – we all need a helping hand*
- *connected to others – it's a chance for them to be generous (and we all love the chance to show kindness to others)*
- *dependent on others – and I value my independence.*

NOTES

Chapter 22

SHAKE THE SILENCE

Words came easily to me.

Apparently, I started speaking when I was nine months old. My older sister was born deaf and couldn't speak. She and I had a special bond that required no language. I was the only one who could understand her. So at nine months, I became her interpreter.

As a child, when our family crowded around the TV to watch *Little House on the Prairie*, I'd watch, then turn to my sister and silently mouth the key plot points.

My sister went through 12 grueling years of speech and hearing therapy to learn to pronounce her *s*'s and *th*'s so she could make herself understood in the world.

When something comes easily, like language did for me, it's natural to take it for granted. When we have never had to struggle or reach for something, we imagine it is our birthright. We don't see it for what it is.

Instead, I have always known how precious words are. How some people have to struggle for them. How painstaking it can be for some people to have a voice. And I have always felt an overwhelming responsibility to use my words well and wisely, and to speak up on behalf of those who cannot speak for themselves. That's why I spent years as a women's rights activist, and I teach people how to write their stories, especially the painful ones.

Many of us can speak. But we have no voice.

We don't speak what is true – perhaps we don't even know what is true for ourselves. And we're afraid of being judged and shamed.

> *What is the source of our first suffering? It lies in the fact that we hesitated to speak....it was born in the moments when we accumulated silent things within us.*
> **GASTON BACHELARD**

When we were small, we might have been taught: children should be seen but not heard. Or we were told we were too loud – told to shut up, be quiet, stop answering back, stop asking so many questions.

If that silence is imposed on us, and if it's the source of suffering, we have a divine obligation to shake the silence, and break it. To find our true voice.

The silences can be huge – familial, cultural, societal, historical, political. In families and in cultures, we inherit silences as well as stories and splinter narratives.

We form ourselves around the gaps and the unsaid things as much as we do around what has been said or is explicit. What is never spoken of, the secrets and taboos, become ghosts that haunt us. They can shape our lives dramatically.

In Chapter 2, we welcomed silence as a nurturer of our inner worlds. But sometimes silence is not nourishing or life-giving. If it has been imposed on us and has robbed us of our story, it can erode our sanity and souls. When we shatter the silence, we choose how and when to speak. We decide what words to fit to dislodge a narrative that has kept us quiet. This chapter is about writing as an act of rupture and rewriting of our stories, this time, in our own voices.

An enforced silence robs us of our story, our sanity and our soul – it can throttle us. Something goes crooked inside of us. The hush grows tightly around us like a forest of thorns around the castle of Sleeping Beauty. Silence becomes an intractable fortress. A moat, a place we cannot cross. This kind of silence happens around topics like menstruation, sexuality, death, because we are erotophobic, homophobic, death-phobic. Silences fester and make truth difficult. This kind of silence can become suffocating. We can become sick.

We certainly cannot live into our true vitality and our true power when we are suppressing the truth, when we remain silent.

So we are called upon to name them, and allow them to be brought into the light so we can integrate them and not play them out in some pathological or repressed form.

AFFIRMATION

There's something I need to say.

Now let's explore the idea of absence, and how absence is also a presence.

A parent or a sibling who dies.

A miscarriage.

A stillbirth.

An accident.

When people disappear from our lives and our ancestral lines, their absence creates its own form of presence. Whatever is missing in our lives becomes a presence – a parent who was unavailable or depressed, a single child who longed for a sibling that never came, or waiting for a proposal or declaration of love that never comes.

The author James Hollis writes in his book *Hauntings:*

> We are haunted by absences – parents who were unavailable, the not-enough-love we never got, things that were missing in our lives and all the other hungers we live with (hunger for conversation, meaning, friendship, joy, insight…).

And,

> Death, divorce and distance do not end relationships. There are more loose ends than we ever repair, and we all bleed somewhere from the raggedy edges of life's unfinished business. All of these absences are presences and play a role in the governance of our lives, whether we know it or not.

Shaking and breaking silence look like:
- speaking up – raising your voice;
- stepping into the spotlight – we can no longer remain invisible, so if we have built a safe world in which we don't take up space, keep a low profile and don't rock the boat, this has to change.

But friends, we have to see and value ourselves enough – so we need conviction and all the other courages we have developed over the past many chapters to shake the silence.

There is another form of silence we don't ever think about as such: toxic politeness.

Edwin Land says, 'Politeness is the poison of collaboration.'

Politeness that excuses atrocity or bad behaviour is a form of censorship.

Women in particular suffer from this malady.
- excusing abusive behaviour,
- cooperating with oppression,
- turning a blind eye to injustice.

The wonderful feminist writer and activist Mona Eltahawy speaks about how we have a 'devotion to the inoffensive.' This disempowers us.

Sometimes breaking a silence will make us unpopular.

It will shatter an illusion.

It might make us a target.

The #metoo movement is the result of women standing up and saying, 'We won't be silent about this anymore.'

Many people who come to me for mentoring to write their stories are rupturing a silence, and what I can tell you is that we feel disloyal when we tell the truth. Sometimes we believe we owe family members or ex-partners the protection of our silence. We don't want to embarrass or humiliate them. We don't want them to be exposed. Our silence shields them.

When we write, we are committing to shaking up a silence within us, to rupturing the void.

As we put words on the page, we start to build a bridge to our own voice.

Without words and language, we are voiceless. Cut off. Alone. Writing connects us inward – and if we share our writing

– to each other, so that we can belong to our own true selves and to this world. Writing is always a sign of life, an indicator of survival. What could be more inspiring and healing than writing, 'I went through some hardship, but look, I survived'?

Martin Niemöller was a Lutheran pastor in Germany who was outspoken against the Nazis. He is best known for this quotation:

> *First they came for the socialists, and I did not speak out – because I was not a socialist.*
>
> *Then they came for the trade unionists, and I did not speak out – because I was not a trade unionist.*
>
> *Then they came for the Jews, and I did not speak out – because I was not a Jew.*
>
> *Then they came for me – and there was no one left to speak for me.*

Breaking the silence is a radical act of solidarity for all others who have been silenced in the same way.

WRITING SKILL

Sometimes we think we're writing one story, and we write and write and we realize long into the process that, in fact, there has been a silent twin, beneath or behind the story we thought we were writing. In fact, what we were writing was simply a form of throat-clearing and we had to do it in order to get to the silence, the quiet understory waiting for us. So writing is sometimes an act of reaching through the explicit, to touch the implicit; of pulling back the veil of what is spoken or articulated, to make contact with the unspoken and unarticulated. Sometimes we have to write in order to unearth a story that really needs to come out, which is hiding beneath or behind.

WRITING EXERCISE

I will no longer be silent about…

REFLECTION QUESTION

Speaking up for myself or others:
- *might make me a target of others' vitriol*
- *terrifies me – I would rather be silent and invisible*
- *is essential to my life force*
- *enlarges my sense of who I am.*

NOTES

Chapter 23

REMAKE YOURSELF

In Cormac McCarthy's book, *All the Pretty Horses,* he writes about a man standing at the window looking out, and thinking to himself that it was just as well that God withheld the truths of life from young people 'else they'd have no heart to start at all.'

All of us get broken by life. Brought to our knees. Hurt beyond the belief that we will heal.

The poet Stanley Kunitz refers to life as 'a feast of losses.'

I used to think this was a flaw in the human experience – like why should we have to suffer so much? Can't we all just live healthily and happily ever after?

It's not easy being a person, is it?

But there isn't an alternative path. We can't avoid the inevitable suffering that comes with being a person. We are born to break.

So, dear friend, you didn't get it wrong, or make a mistake, or choose the wrong path.

The alternative road you imagine you should have taken likely held its own unique anguish. Who knows? It could have been an even greater suffering. When we get lost in this fantasy of what else could have been, it might be a good time to return to Chapter 4 in this book, Nurture What's Here Now.

Sometimes life deals us a blow that feels so catastrophic, so shattering that our sense of ourselves and everything we know splinters into a million pieces.

Just like Humpty Dumpty in the nursery rhyme, we fall off walls – maybe the wall was poorly manufactured, maybe there was an earthquake, maybe we weren't watching where we were going, maybe someone pushed us. It doesn't matter. We all fall down, and we all get broken.

The problem is not being broken.

Humpty Dumpty couldn't get fixed because he roped all the king's horses and all the king's men to put him back together again. He outsourced his healing.

The problem when we break is believing other people can or should fix us.

The right doctors, therapists, gurus, authors or loved ones.

We are the ones who have to take responsibility for remaking ourselves.

Now, of course, we may need medication, rehab, support groups, time out, guidance from teachers, and especially love and support from family and friends. We can and should use everything in our power to find a way to go on.

I am a massive fan of the band Coldplay and have been known to belt out the lyrics to the song 'Fix You' on many occasions. But I'm wary of the message of that song.

Trying to fix someone else is a misunderstanding of how to love someone.

And we give our power away when we expect others to fix us.

The mending, repairing, remaking, reconstitution, that must happen when we break down is a job we must undertake with the support of others as well as the mysterious forces of the unknown.

The Japanese art of Kintsugi is part of the tradition of what is known as Wabi Sabi, the beauty of that which is impermanent, incomplete and imperfect.

A broken vessel is fixed with gold resin so that the fractured place becomes the most beautiful part of the object.

I once did a Kintsugi workshop, and I was amazed to learn that when you fix a vessel in this way, the first thing you do is you exaggerate the broken seam. You file it down, expanding the broken space so that it is large enough to fill with gold resin.

So it's almost like the object is saying, 'Hey look, this is where I am imperfect,' as opposed to hiding the break.

I found this such a beautiful metaphor for human repair of a broken heart.

No-one in this world is walking around fully put together without scars, fractures, stitches – literal or metaphoric.

Every single one of us is working to remake ourselves and reconstitute our frayed, dangly, unlovable bits. Some of us are just doing it more consciously than others.

So those people who seem to have it all together are perhaps just those of us who are consciously remaking themselves, going back time and time again to find their orphans who are on the job of finding medicine for the soul.

A writing practice such as this is an indication of someone remaking themselves.

There is no point at which we can stop doing this work.

It's not like there is an instruction manual, and once we have worked through all the steps, we can say, 'There we go. Now I'm all put back together. I can get back up on that wall.'

The work of integration, making ourselves whole, and repairing lost parts, soothing tender places, comforting abandoned orphans, is never done.

Some days we will feel a little bit more together than others.

Some days we will feel unravelled and impossibly scattered.

That may be a day in which a writing practice might be a gift to your fragmented spirit.

And when you sit down, come with curiosity, compassion, courage and see where the break aches the most. The repair is a product of paying a certain kind of attention to the pain by shining the lantern of one's own consciousness onto that crack.

The gold resin is the attention we bring, the words we find to articulate how and in what way we feel lost, exiled, broken and unloved.

In the words of the Spanish poet, Antonio Machado, we can, 'Make sweet honey from old failures.'

AFFIRMATION

 **Where I am broken is where I am most beautiful.**

Being broken is never the problem.

If it is a problem at all, it is the problem of simply being human.

What causes us to suffer is not being able to feel, articulate and shine loving attention into our wounded places.

As soon as we do, our attention acts like a laser. We can, like in the art of Kintsugi, exaggerate that wound, really feel into the pain; and once we've poured love and compassion into that crack, we find we've created a beautiful scar that speaks not just of pain but all the way in which pain has fired us in the kiln of life and shaped our spirits. Our scars are what make us each unique.

Nothing is stronger than a bone that has been broken and that it resets or remakes itself.

So wherever you are broken and have remade yourself is the place where you are the strongest you have ever been.

And in this way, you become someone others can lean on. Not someone whose job is to fix others, but who can speak about the journey of remaking oneself.

> *Don't turn your head. Keep looking at the bandaged place.*
> *That's where the Light enters you.*
> **RUMI**

Sorrow and grief are surely not just here to rob us of passion and a sense of meaning, but to enable us to live more deeply, more joyously. What we find is in the words of the poet Theodore Roethke: 'In a dark time, the eye begins to see.'

Inside of us is a landscape larger than suffering, larger even than that little word 'happiness' which is a cliché and covers too much ground. Being broken gives us a chance to look life in the eye. To expand the reach of our souls. Beneath the broken heart beats another heart that cannot break, that is large enough to hold all our suffering.

In the midst of tragedy, all the distractions of superficiality fall away. We become deeply attuned to the preciousness of life.

We can feel more awake than we ever have.

Our senses become sharpened, our hearts softened, our clarity about what matters becomes translucent.

And we heal, we heal, crookedly, imperfectly, brokenly. And in healing, we grow and transform.

As Rilke writes in his poem, 'A Man Watching':

This is how he grows: by being defeated, decisively,
by constantly greater beings.
(TRANSLATED BY ROBERT BLY)

Maybe our work is not to become whole, complete, perfect or fixed. Maybe the work of remaking ourselves is simply to be more conscious of our shadows, our ruptures and our dark edges.

I tried to drown my sorrows, but the little bastards learned how to swim, and now I am overwhelmed by this decent and good feeling.
FRIDA KAHLO

This decent and good feeling she speaks of comes from the act of remaking ourselves and stitching ourselves back together.

We do this work:
- simply by bearing witness,
- by naming what has happened to us,
- by collecting the broken pieces,
- by bringing our attention to our wounds.

They tried to bury us
They did not know we were seeds
MEXICAN PROVERB

WRITING SKILL

Whenever we are working on a big piece of writing (an essay, a short story, a book), we work with broken pieces and only later, make something whole of them.

Writing happens in stages – especially when we are writing for a reader.

The first draft comes out in bits and pieces, dribs and drabs. Broken pieces, if you like.

Rewriting is the next step, in which we take the bits and pieces and rework them, put them together, find and make connections, and begin to see an invisible structure that has been quietly forming. This is the way a story starts to take shape.

WRITING EXERCISE

I have remade myself by …

REFLECTION QUESTION

Can you feel the light that enters through your wounded place?
- *no, I still feel exquisitely fragile there*
- *sometimes, fleetingly*
- *I am defended in the places I have been hurt – strong but cynical*
- *I am strongest there because I have remained soft and open.*

NOTES

Chapter 24
CONNECT THE DOTS

*If you wish to make an apple pie from scratch,
you must first invent the universe.*
CARL SAGAN

Everything is connected to everything else in the world.

One of the most unhelpful ideas of Western culture has been the cult of Individualism. Of course, each one of us is unique as a snowflake or a fingerprint, but in thinking of ourselves as special, my fear is that we have overshot the ego by inflating it monstrously.

In so doing, we have forgotten a fundamental principle of quantum physics – that we are all connected.

We have stopped understanding ourselves as part of something greater than ourselves. This has extended into the cult of the personality, and results in us turning people into gurus, which may be one of the least helpful ways we can help ourselves.

In Africa, where I come from, we have our own version of the blessing of *namaste*, which means the light in me sees and honours the light in you. In Africa, we call it *ubuntu*, and it means, 'I am a person through other people. We are humans through other humans.'

The Shona tribe of Zimbabwe has a unique greeting. When someone asks, 'How are you?' you respond, 'I am well, if you are well.'

How did you sleep? I slept if you slept well.

We are in desperate need of the wisdom that resides in traditions that honour the interconnectedness of all things.

One of the greatest social issues we face is that so many of us feel desperately alone. It's bizarre in the age of social media and technology, which supposedly connects us to the world wide web and to thousands, tens of thousands of other people – yet, loneliness is one of the biggest problems we face today.

We suffer desperately when we don't feel connected to other human beings, to life on this planet.

When we find ourselves in this bardo, life can feel meaningless.

Connection is our greatest need. Belonging is our greatest desire.

At times like this, writing can help us reconnect – with ourselves first and foremost, then with others, to all life and to the point of our ongoing existence.

Writing is a conscious act of reconnecting and can reinvigorate us with a sense of meaning and purpose.

As we write, as we pay attention to our inner lives, as we remember, retrieve our orphans, we may begin to feel again. We start to gently pull the tendrils of meaning out from our suffering.

And as we do this, we realize that we are not alone – others are also experiencing this form of suffering.

We begin to feel connected to others – and our sense of

what is possible enlarges.

We become part of a family, a community, a country, the whole of humanity. And then beyond that, we feel a kinship to all living creatures – the birds, the fish, the animals, the trees, the plants. We start to feel a connection to the earth.

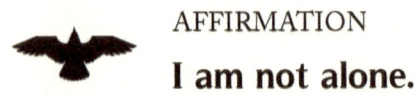

AFFIRMATION
I am not alone.

I now invite you to enlarge the sky inside your heart by connecting more deeply to yourself. Take a moment to sink into yourself and make I-contact.

The deepest, most sacred element of writing is the connection we make – first and foremost with ourselves.

To every one of our senses.

To our bodies.

Our emotions as they rise and subside.

Our memories as they come and go.

Our values and beliefs.

We cannot write if we're anesthetized and numb to our own pain, grief, joy, lust and longing – we have to be in touch with it all.

Now, can you extend that feeling of connection to one other person? Someone you know and love? Gently stretch that connective tissue and draw them close.

Can you feel how their pulse races? How their bodies digest and burp and ache and thirst and feel hunger?

How they too fret and long and pray? How their hearts are also tender? Now, can you extend that feeling of connection to someone you're indifferent to – a stranger, someone you see regularly but you don't know them well, perhaps the person who collects your garbage, your bus driver, the person who delivers your Uber Eats?

Can you see them as just another version of you, living out a life, full of dreams and dramas, hopes and hurts?

Can you now extend that feeling of connection to someone you don't like? Someone you have negative feelings towards?

See them in a moment of vulnerability.

When they've just received bad news.

Struggling for breath.

They too are human just like you.

Now we can extend this connection to the trees, the birds, the koalas, the kookaburras, the stingray, the earthworms, the moss, the rivers, the mountains, and all of life that buzzes and hums and works as hard as we do, to stay alive.

This exercise of connection helps us to see themes – universal experiences – that tie all of us together.

When we write, we begin to see our lives as not separate from everything else that is going on in the world, and we cross the bridge between the personal and the universal.

WRITING SKILL

Writing is an enterprise of making connections and tying threads.

We're always looking for connections, ways in which things can be linked.

The one way to weave different together is by using themes.

Themes are universal notions – they are a tool we use in writing to connect the personal with the universal: love, justice, innocence.

Themes are like echoes or threads that run through our writing. They become a refrain; they help us to make patterns in the narrative. Writing is often a search for patterns – things that are like other things, symbols that repeat, icons that have both personal and universal meaning.

When I write a book, I make a list of the themes I'm exploring, and then I connect and weave objects and characters and scenes that represent that theme.

In my book *Things Without a Name*, one of the themes was the separation of nature from our lives, and a little African violet pot plant becomes a symbol of how Faith, the main character, brings the outside, inside.

Throughlines are these golden threads that run through a narrative that connects disparate parts of our story and creates a feeling of cohesion for the reader.

Kisa Gotami was a young woman in the time of the Buddha. Her only child, a little boy, died tragically and she went out of her mind with grief. An old man took pity on her and told her, 'Go and see the Buddha. He has the medicine that is going to help you bring your child back to life.'

She begged the Buddha to give her the medicine that would bring her son back to life.

The Buddha said, 'I do have the medicine, but in order for me to give it to you, I need you to bring me a back a handful of mustard seeds from any home in which there has been no death.'

Immediately, she ran through the village, knocking on every door.

People wanted to help her, and were only too happy to help her and give her the mustard seeds. But as soon as she asked, 'Have you had any death in your family?' every single person replied, "Yes, I lost my brother. I lost my wife. I lost my father. I lost my daughter.'

And as she went from door to door, her heart opened wide, and she woke from her trance of grief. She recognized that she was not alone, that grief was everywhere, and she was connected to every person who had suffered loss.

She became enlightened and went on to become a great spiritual teacher.

So friends, writing is one way that we can rescue us from catastrophic loneliness and remind us that we are part of the great family of humanity.

As we write our stories, and we connect more deeply with ourselves, we also connect with the pain of others, we become more compassionate and empathic.

We take our place in the great family of all beings.

WRITING EXERCISE

I feel connected to…

REFLECTION QUESTION

Seeing that my life has universal themes:
- *makes me feel connected to all other life on the planet*
- *relieves my loneliness*
- *makes me feel insignificant*
- *I realize I am not special.*

NOTES

Chapter 25
SWITCH

What is healing, but a shift in perspective?
MARK DOTY

When we get stuck in our lives, we may think that if only our circumstances could change, we'd be satisfied, happy, fulfilled. If only we:

- got a new job,
- lost weight,
- fell in love,
- had more money, then all our problems would go away.

But friends, we know, don't we, that that kind of thinking is a trap? It is one of the most common ways we give up our power – by imagining we have no control.

We don't always control our circumstances.

But what if by simply changing where we stand – moving from north to south or from east to west, peering through a different lens – what if any of these maneuvers – all within our power – could give us what we want: happiness, joy, relief, a sense of wellbeing?

Reframing or switching is a spell-breaking tool.

Spells are stories, versions of reality, paradigms, worldviews or a set of beliefs, a way of seeing the world.

A spell breaks when things change irrevocably, not because circumstances change, but because how we see reality, shifts.

We often say that seeing is believing, but a better truth is that believing is seeing.

Today's chapter is about using writing to reframe.

My husband I once had an awful experience when we attended a meeting with a group of parents to discuss a sports tour for our children. They were an impenetrable clique, in the way that these closed groups sometimes form and did not want our son to be part of the tour. They were many, and my husband and I were just two outsiders.

The behaviour that night was some of the ugliest I've ever encountered – cruel, unethical, lacking all compassion. I left there, broken emotionally. The next day, I lost my voice and was sick in bed for days. I couldn't think about that meeting without feelings of rage welling up inside. I had terrible, mean thoughts about all those people, including some who were just too scared to show support for our son and break rank with those who clearly controlled the finances. I was obsessing with outrage, but completely powerless to change the circumstances.

So I took out my journal and I began to write. As the words began to flow, I described each parent as a caricature. I exaggerated the behaviours and enlarged the shadow. They became a cast of ghastly, ludicrous characters. I turned all the subtext into dialogue – the things people really mean to say, but pretend otherwise. And suddenly, I began to laugh. By the end of the writing, the event had lost all its emotional power over me. It became a funny story.

So you see, we can take control of a story instead of allowing the story to control us. We can do this by switching places. By becoming the author, not the victim.

That is the power that reframing has – it can transform and shift our perspective.

The Japanese artist Hokusai painted Mount Fuji. But he realized that one painting of Mount Fuji only showed you one side. So he began to paint many versions of Mount Fuji and his collection, 36 Views of Mount Fuji, was published in Japan in 1830s. He believed that you could only understand the 'inner meaning' of something when you had seen it from many different views.

Similarly, the Chilean poet Pablo Neruda wrote a hundred love poems for his beloved, because what would one poem really say? It would never do justice to her complexity and the fullness of his feeling for her.

> *Until the lions tell their own story, the story of*
> *the hunt will always glorify the hunter.*
> **CHINUA ACHEBE**

This is true of history and all historical accounts.

We must always ask – who is the teller of this tale?

By switching places, we acknowledge that there is no such truth as one size fits all – sexuality, life choices, size, beauty, age, culture.

Reality is kaleidoscopic – the more inclusive our storytelling, the more versions of reality we have, the richer it is for everyone. There is no one story that speaks the whole truth.

The wonderful author Chimamanda Ngozi Adichie has a TED talk called, 'The Danger of a Single Story,' in which she explores this idea, and I encourage you to watch it.

The animal and natural world is alive and has its own intelligence. It's observing us as much as we believe we are the observers.

Michael Polin in *The Botany of Desire: A plant's eye view of the world* asks, 'What if we are the strategy of apples?'

The snow doesn't give a soft white damn whom it touches.
E. E. CUMMINGS

One of the most beautiful books I've read in the past while is called *Braiding Sweetgrass* by Robin Wall Kimmerer. She says 'to name and describe you must first see.'

Her native indigenous language is Potawotami, and it is a language full of verbs. The language includes verbs which, when translated, mean, 'to be a Saturday,' 'to be a hill,' 'to be red,' 'to be a long, sandy stretch of beach,' 'to be a bay.'

In English, non-human things are 'it' as defined by humans. A bay is a noun only if we consider that water is not alive enough to 'be a bay.'

We consider 'being-ness' the exclusive realm of humans.

The verb, 'to be a bay' releases the water from human definition.

Living water has decided to be a bay – it could become a stream, waterfall.

In a world in which everything is alive – water, land, even a day of the week, there is a whole new world of verbs.

When we swap places, we become attuned to the animacy in the world, the life that pulses through all things.

A language that includes the environment changes our relationship with it.

In her book *Gathering Moss*, Kimmerer suggests that when we have a problem in life, we should ask, 'What would moss do?'

 **AFFIRMATION**
I am only oxygen and nitrogen.

When we switch perspective through language, we break the spell of human sovereignty over nature. We can change how we feel about things by changing our language and the way we speak about things. Healing doesn't necessarily happen when circumstances change, but when we change how we feel about circumstances.

Einstein famously said:

There are two ways to live your life – as if nothing is a miracle and as if everything is a miracle.

What's the difference? Just choice of how we look at the world. In science, there is a notion in measurement called the Error of Parallax, which is caused by looking at things at an angle instead of straight on. Depending on where you stand, objects will look closer or further away.

Our position, standpoint, vantage or perspective determines what we see, and therefore, the story we tell.

Shakespeare wrote:

Nothing is either good or bad, but thinking makes it so.

And the British essayist Erich Heller once wrote:

Be careful how you see the world. It is that way.

Writing facilitates these switches in so many ways.

We can use language to:
- zoom in and out – a close-up view but also a long view;
- change places – speak from the perspective of other characters or people who have hurt us;
- make a story funny and find the humour – to remove the sting of our suffering;
- shift points of view and perspective – we can look back, look down from above, using an omniscient perspective as opposed to a subjective one (this we do by changing from first, to second, to third person);
- alter the lens to see what is out of the frame, look from another angle, ask, 'What am I not seeing? What is hidden from view?'

WRITING SKILL

The writing skill for this chapter is to expand the understanding of point of view and perspective.

When we write sentences, we use subjects, verbs and objects.

But what if we allowed the objects to become the subjects?

Instead of us pouring tea from a teapot, what if the teapot pours us?

Instead of putting on our reading glasses, what if our reading glasses put us on?

Here are some poems I wrote when I experimented with this technique:

Housework Poems

The teapot pours me
into the porcelain cup
I flow easily
and let off plenty of steam.

My reading glasses
put me on
and sigh
'Ah, clear at last!'

It's a lot of fun to play around this way, by switching the subjects and objects of our sentences.

WRITING EXERCISE

You have some options here. You can switch your subjects and objects – which is a more lighthearted exercise.

Or if you'd like something a little more emotionally demanding, switch places with someone you have had conflict with. Write about the situation from their perspective.

REFLECTION QUESTION

The greatest gift of changing places in a challenging moment is:
- *my ability to feel compassion for someone else's point of view*
- *less hubris, more humility*
- *letting go of 'being right'*
- *being able to change my mind.*

NOTES

Chapter 26
SEEK THE STORY

Wherever we find ourselves in our lives, we have the power to think of ourselves as being part of a story or better still, of many stories.

And every story has what we call an arc.

An arc is the path or backbone of the story. And it has a particular shape and structure.

A beginning, middle and an end.

Or in writerly speak, exposition, rising action, and climax and a resolution.

A story begins when something new happens or something changes. We call this the inciting event.

Storytelling relies on structure, and there are many shapes a story can take.

I'm inviting you to think of your life as a story and place yourself inside the shape of a story.

Ask yourself, 'What has changed in my life?'

What am I initiating? What am I at the beginning of? What is blossoming? What is seeding? Budding?

There you go – that's your beginning.

Maybe you're in the middle of something?

A phase in your life? Career? A way of thinking? A relationship? An identity?

Maybe you're at the end of something? Something is dying, leaving you, subsiding.

Stories follow a deep structure that is encoded in the human brain.

When we start to put the puzzle together, we begin to see the way in which it all holds itself together.

At the core of this, is the impulse to make meaning.

As humans, we're hardwired to make meaning out of our experiences.

Meaning is not inherent, as Viktor Frankl taught in logotherapy. Logotherapy is a psychotherapeutic approach based on the belief that human nature is motivated by the search for a life purpose.

The pursuit of meaning is an act of creativity on our part, in each moment of our lives.

So when you reflect on your life, how do you understand the hard times you've been through?

What have you made of your childhood?

Of your relationships? Friendships? Lovers?

Your losses?

Your gender? Sexuality? Religion? Humans are meaning-makers. We're wired to wrestle with 'the things that happened' and to shape them away from the arbitrary and capricious.

The stories we tell about ourselves shape who we are.

Have we been a victim of circumstance?

Has everyone just been out to get us?

Have we endlessly floundered in toxic family dynamics, legal battles or non-speaking-terms with various folk?

Do we see ourselves as the good guy or the bad guy?

Do we blame others for where we are?

Are we blessed or cursed?

Are we motivated by revenge, power, money, fame, love, lovingkindness, service?

Are we helpless? Hapless? Unlucky? Powerless?

Or are we blessed, lucky, powerful?

When we think of our lives this way, we start to see patterns.

We always seem to be the victim. Or the rescuer.

The black sheep or the favourite child.

Abandoned or betrayed.

Always on the outside.

A magnet for drama.

Or maybe nothing ever changes.

These patterns or shapes are stories.

In writing about our lives, we shape and own the meaning we are making of our lives. We also determine the legacy we will leave.

Stories ask us to find who we are through the tangle of experience, and to make our own meaning from it all.

In writing, we shape what we have lived and seen.

AFFIRMATION
I make my own meaning.

If you think of your life and everything that has happened to you as a lump of unformed clay and writing as wheel – you place your life on the wheel and you turn it into a shape. You give it shape.

Writing allows us to craft meaning from our experiences.

Distance, perspective and time help us to construct meaning so we can ask: *What really happened here? How did it shape me?*

What do I believe and trust in the light of this?

From this vantage point, we honour the self who endured, the self who survived, and who now stands on the other side of it all, able to look back.

When you reflect on your story, you decide. Is it a:
- drama,
- love story,
- tragedy,
- romance,
- comedy,
- comedy of errors?
- Who are the heroes and villains?
- Where are the crises and dark nights of the soul?
- Where are the beginnings? The middles?
- How does it resolve?

Every story is one of survival, betrayal, a loss of innocence, injustice, bravery, cowardice, cruelty and faith.

But shaping our story relies on our ability to do one important maneuver. Remember how in Chapter 20 we went back for the orphans? We returned to the place where our suffering happened. We felt the pain all over again.

Now I am going to share with you the final step that is crucial for healing.

It's the skill of reflection.

Let's go back to that moment where you returned for your orphans.

Take a moment to go back there. You know how to get there now.

Once you're there, I'd like you to take a few steps back.

Become the third eye. See yourself in that moment but as an observer, from a distance.

Look at yourself surviving that moment. At the time, you didn't know that you would survive; but from afar, you know you did.

Now comes the moment you have been waiting for – what the whole enterprise has been about.

Ask yourself how surviving that moment has impacted your life.

What meaning have you made from that moment?

This is the crucial step. This is where you reflect.

This is what you have come back for – to reflect and make meaning from that moment.

That is where the moment transforms.

All this time, it has been floundering, looking for a place in your psyche, for the chaos to settle, for the fog to lift. That happens when we make meaning.

What meaning you make is entirely up to you. It is personal.

There is no right or wrong meaning.

You decide what that moment meant and how it fits into your life story. You get to say how it has made you the person you've become.

In looking back, what slow-releasing gifts did it give you?

Even trauma, heartache and suffering have meaning.

Now you have returned wiser, stronger, older, to retrieve that meaning.

To weave straw into gold.

WRITING SKILL

Every story has a beginning, middle and end. That's what we call the plot. But as writers, we choose where the beginning and ending are. There is no such thing as the beginning of a story; that is just the choice we make to say, 'Here is where I start.'

'And they got married and lived happily ever after' is the end of a story about two people who fell in love. But it is the beginning of a story about a marriage.

The fact that we are alive and breathing and can ask questions is a privilege and a cause for celebration.

It is the mark of a person remaking herself. It is birth all over again, this time, by choice.

No matter our histories (and let's face it, some of us have survived some hard times), we are free to rechristen our experiences; to declare motherhood a form of leadership, self-love, a weapon of disarmament and storytelling, a superpower.

As soon as we name our experience, we belong to it; and as we share it with others, we take our place in the grand family of humanity.

WRITING EXERCISE

There are many stories you could tell about your own life. Your love stories. Your failures. Your successes. Your passions. Your losses.

Pick any one.

What is the beginning of that story?

Where does it begin?

And where are you now in that story – at the beginning, somewhere in the middle or at the end?

Were you able to place yourself in whatever story you've chosen to write about? Was it easy or tricky for you?

REFLECTION QUESTION

When I feel stuck in my life, I:
- *overgeneralize and imagine, 'This is the end'*
- *know things will change – I am just in the middle of something*
- *look for a new perspective to change the story*
- *try to find a new beginning so I can start over.*

NOTES

Chapter 27

MAKE PEACE

We all carry pain from past experiences.

Sorrow, anger, grief and trauma can cling to us when we've been subjected to negligence, abuse, violence or cruelty from others. No matter how hard we try, it can be difficult to shake ourselves free of these feelings.

As a result, we can become bitter. Resentful. Harbor grudges, hatreds, resentments, vendettas.

Don't we all have people we secretly hope karma will catch up with?

But in the meantime, what is the cost of the weight of our sorrow, anger, grief and jealousy? What interest is it extracting from our life-force? We may have obsessive thoughts and keep returning to an encounter or moment, unable to let it go.

But this corrodes our joy.

It dims our vitality. It compromises and clips the wings of our wholeheartedness and delight in the world.

This is not a way for us to live.

Maybe we can take some responsibility for how things transpired, but it's likely we had none or very little control over what happened.

So we're left with what we do have control over.

And that, my friends, is to forgive.

Whatever we cannot forgive, keeps us hostage. Nelson

Mandela famously said, 'As I walked out the door towards the gate that would lead to my freedom, I knew if I didn't leave my bitterness and hatred behind, I'd still be in prison.' Resentment and bitterness erode our life force.

Let me offer this about the practice of forgiveness:
1. Some acts and behaviours are unforgivable. Inexcusable. Whether something is forgivable is not judged by an objective standard – you can decide whether an act is forgivable or not. This has nothing to do with the law, or social norms – you are the judge. Forgiving someone for doing something unforgivable does not excuse, condone or make what they did okay.
2. The person may be dead, or you may not be in touch with them. They do not need to know that you are forgiving them. You are forgiving them as an act of mercy and kindness to yourself. So that you can be free. It has nothing to do with them.
3. Forgiveness allows us to move forward and stop holding on to a story that is weighing us down and keeping us stuck.

Many of the people who I mentor are writing memoirs and are writing about family members and other people who have treated them very poorly. We always discuss how to write about others, because that is the hardest part of writing our stories – how to write honestly about an experience that involves another person, when that person has not consented to you writing about them.

I have an unusual approach to this, which I call, The Hygiene of Writing About Others.

- The first step is to write freely and without censorship. If you're angry, write angry. If you're full of hatred, write it all down. Do not think about whether what you're writing is hurting anyone. There must be complete catharsis – you must let it all out. Call the person names, use profanities, feel everything you feel. Really go there. Give it all you've got – full throttle.
- But then, step away. Once you've got it all down, put space between you and that piece of writing. Do not look at it or come back to it for a couple of days or weeks. Really let it rest on the page. Let the page hold it all for you.
- Then when you feel ready and once the writing has had a chance to settle, now you come back to it. Read it aloud so you can hear what it sounds like. Listen to the words. Imagine the words being 'heard' in the world – not just by you, but by others.
- Switch – change places – now read it aloud as if you were standing in their shoes. Imagine them reading or hearing these words spoken.
- Once you've had a chance to feel what the words sound like, not just for yourself, but as if you were hearing it through their ears, invoke the person we're writing about from a soft place inside ourselves. The way to do this is to close our eyes and think about the person we're writing about.

Now try to see them not as the person who hurt us, but as someone who is also suffering. Bring your energy towards that person from your heartspace and say aloud:

> *Your actions caused me untold pain and suffering. Because of what you did, my life has been forever impacted.*
>
> *I want you to know that I forgive you for the pain and suffering you caused me. I recognize that you acted from your own place of woundedness. And I forgive you. May you be well, may you be at peace, may you be free from suffering.*

The aim here is to access compassion for the person, and to release yourself from the psycho-active emotions that their behaviour left in you.

So it's not to erase the memory of what happened, but to neutralize the emotional hold the memory has on you. You are literally offloading a weight. That is the only purpose of doing this exercise. To free yourself.

If you're writing a memoir, which might be published, this would be the right time to rewrite and see what you want to include in a manuscript that will be read by others.

If we were children when these things happened to us, we are necessarily powerless and at the mercy of adults. But we are returning to the 'scene of the crime' as adults now, and making meaning. So we can bring that perspective into the writing.

WRITING SKILL

What is wonderful about writing is that we can imagine an apology we never got. We can write a conversation in which we heal, forgive, let go; and we can experience the release and relief.

Imagine. Write fiction. Make it up.

WRITING EXERCISE

Write a scene that never happened, but create an emotion that you can feel, like I did with the story about those awful parents in the previous chapter.

When we write and shape our stories, we are putting our experiences in order. We're arranging and adjusting our lives, making meaning and creating order out of chaos.

Now sometimes the person we most have to forgive is ourselves. We may have made a mistake or hurt someone – intentionally or unintentionally. We may have committed a crime, been neglectful, cruel, been a bully, betrayed someone, stolen, taken a life. And we cannot let it go.

- The first story I would encourage you to write is the one where you write freely and without censorship. Call yourself names, insult yourself, be as angry and as disappointed in yourself as you like. Call yourself a fool, an idiot, a good-for-nothing, a thug, a loser.
- Then read it aloud. Hear the words that you want to say to yourself.
- Once you've had a chance to feel what the words sound like, close your eyes and invoke the person you were when you made this mistake. Do this from a soft place inside yourself. Can you see that person – not as a terrible human being or a waste of space – but as someone who was suffering at the time. Perhaps we didn't know any better. Maybe we didn't love or value ourselves enough; we didn't have role models or a support structure. We had no-one to help us. We were lost. We were young and immature. We were vulnerable. Can you forgive the person you were for that unforgivable mistake?

Bring your love towards that version of yourself – he or she is just an orphan you have come back for. And say aloud:

> *What you did caused others untold pain and suffering. Because of what you did, their lives, as well as my life, have been forever impacted.*
>
> *But I want you to know that I forgive you for the pain and suffering you caused. I recognize that you acted from your own place of woundedness. And I forgive you. May you be well, may you be at peace, may you be free from suffering.*

AFFIRMATION
We all make mistakes.

WRITING EXERCISE

Think about someone who has caused you pain – a third party or yourself. And your writing prompt is: 'I forgive you for…'

How do you feel after that writing exercise?

REFLECTION QUESTION

How does it make you feel to forgive yourself for past mistakes?
- *like I'm letting myself off the hook*
- *free at last from guilt*
- *vulnerably human*
- *compassionate for the person I once was.*

NOTES

Chapter 28
OFFER THANKS

As soon as I wake up, I check my Garmin to see how many hours I've slept. It gives me a report: Poor, Fair, Good or Excellent Sleep, with a little spiel like, ' Shorter than ideal. Interrupted,' or 'Long and refreshing.' Invariably, my first thought of the day is, 'Damn, I didn't get enough sleep.'

I then look at my day, and try to work out how I'm going to get a swim in, on top of Pilates, or go grocery shopping. I almost always feel as if I don't have enough time to do everything I want to fit into the day.

Lynne Twist in her book, *The Soul of Money*, writes that we rush through our day complaining and worrying about 'not having enough' – whether it's love, money or time. Before we get out of bed, we already feel as if we're behind, inadequate or lacking. We then go to bed at night thinking about all the things we didn't get done that day. Our lives are dominated by this mindset of scarcity which she says 'lives at the very heart of our jealousies, our prejudice and our arguments with life.'

When we live in the shadow of scarcity, we feel stress, anxiety, anger, resignation and envy. Cynicism takes over – we feel as if nothing ever goes right for us, people are just out to get us, nothing ever works out for us, people will always disappoint us or abandon us. This can cause us to feel victimized. We wonder,

'Why is this happening to me? I don't deserve this. Why me?'

Scarcity mentality takes over our whole lives; and we feel as if we don't have enough, we aren't enough, we can't keep up.

The antidote for this ailment of the soul is a practice of giving thanks.

We can use our writing to engage our feelings of gratitude.

If the only prayer you said was thank you, that would be enough.
MEISTER ECKHART

Look, it's easy enough to say thank you when a waiter delivers our coffee, a friend does us a favour or a partner gives us a gift. We're accustomed to saying it reactively, in response to a particular outcome. If we've been waiting for test results, the outcome of an application, donation, grant, award, treatment, news, and we get the result we want – we say thank you.

But what happens when we don't 'get' something first, or we don't get the result we hoped for?

We tend to regard gratitude transactionally – I get something; therefore, I am grateful.

But here are some other ways we can engage gratitude.

We can use it pre-emptively and give thanks for what we don't yet have.

What if we asked for help when we need it, and at the same time, said, 'Thank you, for whatever will be – thy will be done.' We can pre-empt the result by saying thank you in advance? The trick, of course, is to remain unattached to the outcome.

We can also use gratitude as a lens or a frame. It could act as an attitude or mentality we adopt to life. When we look at the world this way, we appreciate what there already is, not what we don't have. We focus on what is already here. This alone creates a feeling of abundance. What we focus on seems to grow. So if we focus on what we have, we feel as if we have more.

We can also act as if there is nothing missing, nothing lacking – in our lives or in ourselves.

And we can stay in gratitude to expand our hearts. If you have kids, perhaps you know that feeling – when you've already got one, and are expecting another one, you can't imagine that your heart could grow anymore to accommodate another whole human being. But what we find is that the heart can grow infinitely. No matter how many children, friends, pets, sunrises, meals – our hearts can always grow bigger. The same is true when desserts arrive after you've stuffed yourself on a meal. You think, 'I don't have space for another mouthful.' But, oh, there we go – we manage to always find space.

Gratitude is just an expression of the expansion we feel – that sense of infinite possibility, of abundance and fullness, where your heart feels so full you can't imagine it being fuller. But what we find is that it can reach further.

The task of a mature human being is to hold grief in one hand and gratitude in the other and be stretched larger between them.
FRANCIS WELLER

Gratitude engages a sense of abundance and generosity towards everything that sustains and supports us.

AFFIRMATION
I am grateful for whatever will be.

WRITING SKILL

This atunement to abundance is a great resource for writers – we have to write knowing that there is always more where that writing came from. If we imagine we are writing from a limited resource of creativity, we will become miserly with our output. We might even become constipated and fear that we are using it up or giving too much away.

We have to write and feel free to delete what we've written, knowing we can always fill up our writing wells again.

This sense of abundance flows from gratitude.

If we can give thanks for whatever will be, without attachment to the outcome, we turn thank you into a form of prayer. A prayer of letting go. A prayer of surrender.

Whenever I feel the need to complain – about a faulty product or poor service – I always lead with thanks. I start with, 'Thank you for delivering this so promptly. Thank you for taking the time to read this email. Thank you for your consideration.' Then when I express my dissatisfaction, the edge is soft. This habit helps us to have fewer ugly encounters. We set the tone – one of respect and dignity – for the person on the other end of a call or email.

Because what I have found is that people are so under-thanked.

We can always find something to say thank you for.

If someone gives us difficult feedback, and it hurts, we can say, 'Thank you for your honesty.'

If someone betrays us, we can privately thank them for showing us the truth of who they are and for giving us the chance to learn something new about ourselves.

If something we wanted desperately doesn't happen, we can give thanks for the universe showing us how badly we really wanted it. Sometimes this is the only way we learn how hungry we are for something, and it fortifies our determination not to give up.

Gratitude is protective, like a vitamin, an immunity booster. It's an effervescent for the soul, a mood enhancer. It lowers our cortisol or stress hormones and apparently, can even help us stay fit and healthy.

Gratitude as a frame is perceptual. It acts as an interpretive device, and the thing is, it is an excellent agent for recruiting other positive emotions. We feel calmer, oxytocin levels go up, and we feel more loving and connected to everyone and everything.

It's a good practice not to compare ourselves to others – but that applies only when we're comparing upwards, when comparison makes us feel deprived or somehow less than. When we compare ourselves to others who have less, we can activate gratitude for what we have. We stimulate feelings of abundance.

We can do this by:
- writing in a gratitude journal;
- paying it forward;
- praying;
- pausing to notice beauty. Gratitude is the pause we take between moments. It's the way we stop and listen, look, feel, experience the world. It's the singe of aliveness;
- praising the ordinary – this acts as an antidote to grief.

When one has nothing left make ceremonies out of the air and breathe upon them.
CORMAC MCCARTHY

We can give thanks for the little things as well as the big things:
- Thank you – the plane landed safely.
- The cancer is not in her lungs.
- It's only three months til I see him.
- I get to celebrate another year.
- We got through that fight.
- I can still swim even if I can't walk.
- I can still eat even if I can't swim.
- I can still taste the honey.
- I can smile.
- I can still hold your hand.

The year I turned fifty, I undertook a ritual.

I spent the year writing handwritten letters of thanks to every single person who has made a difference in my life. I wrote eighty-three letters to old schoolteachers, friends, boyfriends, people I've worked with over my lifetime. It was quite a job to track them down, but I wanted to honour every person who has impacted my life in a positive way. I even wrote letters to people I have subsequently fallen out with, but who meant something to me a long time ago, to thank them for the time we had as friends or lovers. I repaired many relationships in the process. One person had died, so I sent the letter to her parents. It was such a wonderful ritual, and though I was thanking other people, at the end of it all, I felt enlarged. Gratitude is also a way of remembering, and it colours memory with love and forgiveness.

> I sat, a solitary man,
> In a crowded London shop,
> An open book and empty cup
> On the marble table-top.
>
> While on the shop and street I gazed
> My body of a sudden blazed;
> And twenty minutes more or less
> It seemed, so great my happiness,
> That I was blessed and could bless.
>
> **W B YEATS**

WRITING EXERCISE

I am blessed because…

REFLECTION QUESTION

My preferred method of thanksgiving is to:
- *thank those who help and support me*
- *pay it forward*
- *take care of others*
- *pray or meditate.*

NOTES

Chapter 29
TELL THE WHOLE HOLY TRUTH

We try to be honest, but we often fail.

We carry lies in our bodies, even if we don't speak them outright.

> *In the struggle for survival, we tell lies.*
> **ADRIENNE RICH**

We obscure the truth when we deny the longings of our spirits and instead follow paths others have laid out for us. We do this so as not to disappoint them.

We waste time and energy on things that are irrelevant to our soul's sustenance.

We allow people to believe we love them when we do not feel the same. We allow people to believe they mean nothing to us when we love them desperately.

We contort ourselves to fit others' needs.

We make excuses to save face. We cover up the truth because we're trying to protect people, or ourselves. We hide the facts out of shame, not only to others but to ourselves.

We follow rules we don't believe in.

We make sacrifices that feel unbearable and resent those who need us.

We watch people behave wrongly and keep silent, knowing

that our disapproval would cost us our popularity with them.

We stay too long in relationships that are bad for us and give up too easily on others that promise fulfilment.

We eat foods we know make us unwell, we don't drink enough water, and then we berate our bodies for their frailty. We fight battles we know we cannot win, and we don't intervene in others we know we could.

We actively work to keep our own truths concealed from ourselves.

We may be avoiding the truth so as not to cause pain – to ourselves or others.

And we may fear that if we tell the truth, something will have to change.

We may also not feel safe or secure enough to voice the truth.

Living like this can make us sick – at a soul level as well as physically.

When we lie, we are in Mary Oliver's words, 'breathing just a little and calling it a life.'

On the other hand, when we come clean and tell the truth:
- we gain self-respect;
- we can stop hiding and pretending;
- we can relax – because to lie, you have to have a good memory;
- we recover personal authority;
- we like ourselves more – maybe even love ourselves;
- cognitive dissonance dissolves – we don't feel split anymore;
- we feel authentic – because we've embraced the shadow energies that we've been suppressing;

- we become more visible to ourselves and others;
- we feel free, liberated, lighter.

This is because we have honoured the call of our souls and become whole. We're not fragmented anymore.

In this chapter, we are going to write to tell the whole holy truth.

But the first truth you have to know is that it is a lie that there is such thing as The Truth.

There is only the truth of our experience in any given moment.

With every breath, with every passing second, things can change. Our worlds can change, our hearts and minds can change, so the truth is only a moment of authenticity and honesty.

Telling the truth might simply be:
- an act of courage to say, '*I am not happy,*' or '*This isn't good enough,*' or '*Hell, this is not enough of a life for me*';
- dissolving the border between binary ideas – either / or;
- embracing paradox and contradictions (we stop sublimating and making excuses);

Do I contradict myself? Very well then, I contradict myself.
I am vast, I contain multitudes.
WALT WHITMAN

- acknowledging and embracing shadow energies;
- thinking more holographically and looking more deeply at our motivations and hidden stories.

As we write truthfully, we go deeper with a lantern, a shovel, and a big brave heart and begin to feel the safety of our own deepest voice emerging.

Writing the whole holy truth is an act of immense courage as we enter a new conversational territory with ourselves. We listen closely and discover levels of consciousness and knowing that we have not yet tapped.

When we do this, we step outside of our mediocre, clichéd scripts.

When we tell the whole holy truth, we are looking for volume, layers and complexity. We know there are shadows that must be integrated.

Once we do this work on ourselves, we can then extend compassion and empathy to others.

This is where our writing practice comes full circle, back to self-compassion, back to taking responsibility, and to a powerful appreciation of how the personal is by its nature, universal.

AFFIRMATION

 **I own it all.**

WRITING SKILL

Many of us write in clichés – these are just other people's thoughts and experiences. When something comes too easily or is glib, it's very likely a cliché.

The antidote to cliché is to look for the ambivalence or paradox in the experience. We can ask:

What am I not seeing? What is not obvious? What is hidden or buried here?

Our truths involve some pairing of contradictions and the way in which we hold them.

'I am a loving mother,' is only one side of the truth. Or 'I am a terrible mother.'

'He is a selfish narcissist,' likewise.

'She is a dutiful daughter.'

Here are some guidelines for writing the whole holy truth:
- Remember, our truths are always evolving. As soon as we think we know something about ourselves, we change, we transform, and the unknowable part of ourselves is re-established once more. So the truths about our lives are always in motion;
- Our opinions are not our 'truths' – I am not particularly interested in peoples' opinions and I seldom have any of my own. Instead, I'm interested in peoples' stories. Stories are always open-ended, and people can change and become new. An opinion is a position we take. We stake territory with an opinion, and it is often oppositional to other opinions. A story is holographic, an invitation for someone to enter – and they can enter from any number of directions.

Truths are more likely to be found in Rumi's field:

Out beyond notions of me and you is a field, will you meet me there?
RUMI

- Our truths are always contextual, complex, paradoxical;
- Our truths don't dabble in absolutes, clichés or sentimentality;
- When we use words like 'always' and 'never,' we can ask: is this always true?
- Our truths are probably not the first words we write – but our first thoughts offer us gateways to go deeper;
- If something is not grounded in our own felt experience or emotion, it cannot be our truth;
- If it feels scary to say out loud and it makes us feel emotionally raw, we're heading in the right direction;
- If it's a cliché, it may be a cop-out;
- Our truths are not sentimental. Sentimentality can be a distortion, a dishonesty because it warps and tries to deny or flatten the paradox of experience. If we only look in one direction or one dimensionally, we can never tell the truth. Experience is always complex, so our truths must necessarily reflect that;
- If our truths are sentimental, we may be romanticizing (and suppressing something);
- If it feels risky and our heart is racing or it doesn't make 'sense' – we're likely in truth territory;
- If it's only one thing (great, awesome, tragic, desperate), we may want to examine it again. Every truth has depth and complexity. All things have a shadow side. A clue about the truth of our experience is that it is never one thing;
- Overstatements, exaggeration for the sake of exaggeration are not our truths.

The exciting part about owning our truths is that this practice will lead us to our authentic writing voice. This means we will often be engaged in a difficult conversation with something we don't quite understand.

The self that is complete has integrated ambivalence and paradox, and is comfortable with things not quite making sense because they are not one thing or another but both, or many, or at odds: ordinary and miraculous. It's the '*and*,' not the '*or*' maneuver. Romantic and dreary. They hold both grief and lightness. It's this exertion of holding two things that don't belong together that creates a heart space of inquiry. We drop out of one dimension. We see through many dimensions. We don't flatten; we expand;

- And most importantly, when we tell the truth, we 'come home.' We no longer feel exiled and alone. Writing the truth is a pathway to coming home to ourselves. Even when we feel as if we do not belong – to a family, community, tribe or country, we can always belong to ourselves. As human beings, we are part of the great family of life on this planet, and are welcomed each day – by the sun, the sky, water and food. Writing helps us to make a sanctuary where we are and how to belong to ourselves. Home may never be a physical place for us, but it is a place we can cultivate inside ourselves.

WRITING SKILL

The writing tip for today is that when we write our truth, we find our authentic voice.

Our truth is never a cliché.

It is never one-dimensional.

Our truth is not a platitude, nor is it a romanticized or catastrophized version of events.

We can find our truth by entering through many doorways.

WRITING EXERCISE

What is true for me in this moment is… and also…

REFLECTION QUESTION

Owning the truth of my life:
- *makes me afraid no-one will love me*
- *allows me to come out from hiding*
- *releases me from shame*
- *I can embrace the full, glorious, flawed beauty of my soul.*

NOTES

Chapter 30
MAKE HOPE A HABIT

Sometimes if you act as if you will be blessed, you will be blessed.
URSULA LE GUIN

You have made it to the final pages of this book, hopefully, with 29 writing practices undertaken along the way.

That is no small accomplishment.

You have kept returning, kept pitching up. These are the actions that build muscle, wire synapses and exhibit devotion.

You have tended to the fires of your healing and creativity.

You have kept it alive.

In so doing, you've developed a resilience by the mere fact that you have come back to keep writing.

In Sanskrit, there's a beautiful word, *Bhavana*, which means to 'cultivate.'

It's the energy of tilling the fields, allowing them in the right time to lie fallow in anticipation of planting. It's the pruning of the trees in the right season, the oiling of the machinery, the preparation of the space before the work happens.

It's a quiet behind-the-scenes labour that creates a fertile environment for flow.

This is never a once-off. A 'one and done.'

It's an attitude towards our work and an application to the tasks that are asked of us.

When we devote ourselves to any practice, we channel our attentiveness and our focus in a regular way.

Devotion doesn't depend on being in the mood, or feeling like it. It's pitching up no matter what. It's how we honour what we do and how we ensure it becomes part of our lives. It is the antithesis of fickleness and is a display of deep loyalty.

That is what a habit is – a display of ongoing loyalty.

WRITING SKILL

I bring myself to the page every day. Whether it's to catch a dream first thing in the morning, offer thanks, ask for help, recall a moment, capture a moment of awe or try to work out a solution to an emotional problem; and over the years, it has become as unremarkable a daily exercise, like brushing my teeth. I don't think of brushing my teeth as a habit. I'm not in the habit of brushing my teeth. I do it every day without even thinking about. It's like taking out the garbage, doing my laundry – it has become part of the fabric of my being.

The difference between a habit and a practice is that a habit is a repetitive action of the same thing over and over again, without any anticipation that one will become better at the job. I still brush my teeth in the same way I have always done.

But with a practice, with a burgeoning intimacy and depth, we begin to create a relationship with that practice which starts to change us. We may 'get better' at it – in the sense that we begin to use language in new and exciting ways. We are able to truly express the complexity of an experience. We may even find that we feel ready to share some of our writing with others.

It is my conviction that writing is ultimately a practice of hope, even if it just begins as a habit. It is how we declare our intention to grow, transform and work intentionally with our humanity.

Even when we write about our despair, even when we write into our pain and our grief – writing is how we bind hope to what feels hopeless. It is how we sow strength into our weakest places. It is how we stay open to life when all we want to do is contract and disappear.

By continuing to engage with your writing as a habit, it will become a practice; and as you deepen into your practice, you will start to hear the whispers of your own writing voice.

It will emerge, like a polaroid developing, through the intimacy that you develop with your own writing.

So, friends, thank you for the time you have shared with me in these pages.

I want to encourage you to continue to write often and a lot. Daily if you can. Just three minutes a day.

Read too – as much as you can, and different things.

Find writers you love, and let their words stir you and excite you to write more.

It is only by repetition, returning, reworking, recommitting that we begin to heal, grow, stretch and soften.

AFFIRMATION
I will keep coming back.

Writing is a radical act of hope.

When we commit words to the page, we cast our deepest longings for humanity into the world, and we reassert what is good and right about being human.

I hope you will continue this journey, not just for your own sake, but for the sake of a better world that we know is just beyond our reach.

If we deepen into our hearts, we can almost sense the souls of the future looking down on us and imploring us to take responsibility for all life that will come after us.

Let us make our lives sacred by holding in consciousness that everything we touch, everything we do, every word we utter – is not only for ourselves – but for those who must walk ahead of us, those who are as yet unborn, who are relying on us to sow the seeds of the future on their behalf, to plant the trees that will give them shade and bear them fruit.

We are not here *for* ourselves.

We are here *as* ourselves. We are here for others. For those who will make their home in the places we leave behind.

Let us create good habits, practices of compassion, restraint, community, interdependence, patterns of tenderness and gentleness.

We remind ourselves of this with the words we place on the page.

Hope is not some fluffy, feel-good emotion we dust off when we're in despair. It is a practice. A shield. An inclination of the heart. A way of speaking. A way of living. A flourish of the soul. It is how we show up – with the intention of bringing light to dark places, tenderness to suffering.

* * *

I invite you now to close your eyes and feel into your body.

Feel into your exhaustion, anxiety, grief, longing, indifference; feel into the fire, the changings tides of your moods, curiosities. After this thirty-day writing practice, do you feel softer? Less brittle? More open? Kinder? Less constricted?

Has the fist of your heart unclenched, even just a little?

Have you found some silliness in the seriousness of your life?

Have you surprised yourself with how interesting, unpredictable, malleable, generous and forgiving you are?

My hope is that you have stumbled upon your depths, heard the whispers of your soul and that you will carry some of these insights with you as we finish together on this journey and that you may choose writing as your companion, a reliable and loyal friend on your spiritual and healing path.

It is always there for you.

You are always there for you.

You, my dear friend, are your own medicine.

May you be well, may you always be well.

WRITING EXERCISE

My deepest hope...

REFLECTION QUESTION

I practice hope in my life by:
- *never giving up*
- *continuing to learn and grow*
- *giving people second, third and fourth chances*
- *giving myself endless chances to become who I was born to be.*

NOTES

ACKNOWLEDGEMENTS

When my book *Unbecoming* (Lusaris, 2020) was released during Covid, my dear friend Anna Kellerman offered to host a handful of people in her home so I could promote it.

There I met Nadine Richardson, who bought some of my books including *Meditations and Visualizations for Writers and Aspiring Authors* (Joanne Fedler Media, 2019). She asked if I had a course on Insight Timer – which I did not. She then offered to introduce me to the team, and it wasn't long before I was creating my 30-day course, Writing as Medicine for the Soul.

Every week, new students enrol on the Insight Timer app, leaving me comments and questions. I am so appreciative of the chance to share my teaching there. I am grateful to the organizing principles of Life which coalesced to bring Anna, Nadine and the Insight Timer team together to help me produce this course.

Thanks to my wonderful assistant Norie Enn Libradilla for her meticulous and careful editing of this text; to Ida Jansson of Amygdala Designs for the layout and to Rose on 99 designs for the beautiful cover.

I look forward connecting with you if you have any questions.

Just reach out to me at joanne@joannefedler.com. I always answer.

If you'd like to take any of my online writing courses,

- *7 Tricks to Writing Your Story*
- *The Author Awakening Adventure*
- *Write Your First Draft Masterclass*

you can find them all at www.joannefedler.com

www.ingramcontent.com/pod-product-compliance
Lightning Source LLC
Chambersburg PA
CBHW030258100526
44590CB00012B/434